# *Augustinian Studies*

### Papers Read at Recent Augustinian Educational Conferences

61829

*Essay Index Reprint Series*

First published 1937
Reprinted 1967

*Nihil Obstat:*

                     THOMAS F. ROLAND, O.S.A.,
                                *Censor Deputatis.*

*Imprimi Potest:*

                     MORTIMER A. SULLIVAN, O.S.A.,
                                 *Prior Provincialis.*

*Nihil Obstat:*

                     ARTHUR J. SCANLAN, S.T.D.,
                                 *Censor Librorum.*

*Imprimatur:*

                     ✠ PATRICK CARDINAL HAYES,
                                 *Archbishop of New York.*

*Feast of Christian Doctrine, October 3, 1937.*

# CONTENTS

# SAINT AUGUSTINE, THE CHRISTIAN SCHOOLMAN
## AN IDEAL, A STANDARD

IN order to speak intelligently of the work of Saint Augustine as a Schoolman it will be well to recall a few facts to serve as a background of history. These facts will show us some main features of intellectual life in the Church, and help us to keep in mind what was the character of the Christian culture of the time.

The seventy-six years of Saint Augustine's life are years that rank high in the history of Christian culture. For convenience of study we may take a period of less than one hundred and twenty years, from the year A. D. 348, when Saint Cyril delivered his Catechetical Lectures in Jerusalem, six years before Augustine was born, to the year of the death of Pope Saint Leo I, in 461, thirty-one years after the death of Augustine. During these one hundred and thirteen years, which would be easily within the memory of a father, a son and a grandfather in one family, we find that fourteen of the great Fathers and liturgically, *Doctors* of the Church lived and did their work.

The fourteen, with the year of their death, are Hilary of Poictiers who died in 368—Athanasius of Alexandria, died in 372 or 373—Basil the Great, in 379—Cyril of Jerusalem, in 386—Gregory of Naziansus, in 390—Gregory of Nyssa in 395—Ambrose of Milan, in 397—John Chrysostom, in 407—Jerome at Bethlehem in 420—Augustine at Hippo, in 430—Cyril of Alexandria in 444—Peter Chrysologus, in 450—Pope Leo I, in 461.

When Augustine came into the Church in the year 387 there was no immediate demand for the work of his genius in what we may call the field of the Church's Theology. The facts and the meaning of the Catholic Creed were secure. The living Apostolic Tradition of Faith in the Trinity of God and the Word made Flesh had been consistently explained by the earlier thinkers of the fourth century and the third. These fundamentals of our Faith were held as definitely and as intelligently at the close of the fourth century as they are today.

It is evident, I believe, from a study of Augustine's work during the first four or five years of his life as a Catholic layman, that he had no thought of rising to a place of authority in the Teaching Church. Humanly speaking his genius was not needed in the field of the theology of the Church during the closing years of the fourth century. It was only a peculiar twist of heresy in the Donatist factions, later on, that called for a further explanation of the old theology on the nature and the constitution of the Church, and the efficacy of the Sacraments. These Augustine developed when there was urgent call for development. Again, it was the rise of humanistic Pelagianism and its propaganda in North Africa after the first decade of the fifth century that made necessary the action of Augustine and the action of the Church to define the nature and the need of divine grace and the freedom of human choice and will under the influence and the action of God's grace. These facts were independent of Augustine's planning.

It is equally clear, I believe, that the plan of Augustine during these first years of his life in the Church was to live the life and to do the work of a schoolman.[1] The term schoolman is used here in a wide sense of the word. It is meant to indicate only that the matter and the form of Augustine's work were the matter and the form of the work of the schools.

A list of Augustine's written works during those early years in the Faith is like a *topical index* to a textbook in the philosophy of the fourth century. The principles and the main outlines of that philosophy have not changed. *The Laws of Thought, the Groundwork of Knowledge, The Epistemology* of our modern textbooks have elaborated no new principles since Augustine made his first Christian Classical study of Theoretic Skepticism. The three books *Contra Academicos,* if they were turned into idiomatic English, would be a standard of logic and right thinking, and the pride of any school that could produce them or repeat them.

Aside from such a list of Saint Augustine's school studies,

---

[1] Placuit ei, percepta gratia, cum aliis civibus et amicis suis Deo pariter servientibus, ad Africam et propriam domum agrosque remeare—et presentes et absentes sermonibus ac libris docebat.—Possidius—*Vita—cap. III.*

which may be reduced to the place of convenient footnotes, I choose to limit our study here to a few points in Augustine's practice in school work. These points are chosen, *first,* because they are facts in the life of Augustine; *secondly,* because they represent what I believe to be characteristics of Augustine's work as a schoolman. The purpose here is to show, first, that the work of Augustine during the early years of his life in the Church was planned for school use; and secondly, that Augustine's method of teaching is a way of right thinking which does not change with the changing environments of time. The form of right thinking, the premises and conclusions of Augustine's reasoning are right according to the laws of human thought. They are as strong, as vigorous and as convincing now, in the twentieth century as they were in the fourth.

The courses in philosophy taught in the schools of the empire of the fourth century, when Augustine came into the Church, were in some points not unlike the courses that are taught in our non-Catholic Universities at the present time.

Accumulated knowledge and information about the systems of the ancient thought were taking the place of a discerning study and a right judgment on the objective value and the worth of these systems. The result was what we call academic snobbery and theoretic skepticism. There was no fixed plan for right thinking, no philosophy of life.

Here was work to be done in the field of education. It was work for which Augustine was fitted by nature and by more than twelve years of training and experience in teaching. It can be shown, I believe, that Augustine took up this work with vigor and understanding. The three books *Contra Academicos* are, as I see them, the first and the clearest evidence of Augustine's aims, and his plan to build up a new system of education—a system of right thinking, and of reasoning on the facts of the objective world and human experience which we shall find, if we study, was acceptable to the schools of the empire, and sound also on fundamentals and principles where these touch higher truths of revealed religion.

These three books were begun and finished while Augustine

was preparing for baptism in the country seat of Verecundus the Schoolman outside Milan. At the same time Augustine was working on the studies contained in the two books *De Ordine*, the two books of *Soliloquies* and the Ethics of Contentment—*De Beata Vita*. These studies, eight in all, were completed between the late summer months or the early autumn of the year 386 and Easter time of the following year, 387, when Augustine was baptized at Milan.

This school work of Augustine has, I believe, no precedent in the history of education.

It was meant to reform, to put new life, Christian life into the old systems. The same is true of the four or five years which followed, from the time of his baptism, to the time of his ordination to the priesthood, probably in 392. There is of course no material gage to measure influences in educational work. Evidences of these influences must be gathered from texts and the context of the works written during those years, and from references and allusions made to them in letters of personal correspondence with friends, that is, with schoolmen who were interested in the same projects for educational reform; they will be found also in the explicit approval of these early writings contained in his later works, when Augustine was recognized as a guide and teacher in the higher truths of revealed religion and the Faith; and all this is finally reaffirmed in the summary of the *General Review*, which he made of all his writings during the last two years of his life.

I shall quote here briefly from Augustine to make it clear to us what Augustine thought and what he said about the educational system of his time, and about his own plan, which, I insist, is contained in the whole context of the early school treatises. By educational system I mean the government schools of the empire including the provinces.

It is worthy of note, I believe, and a fact to be marked, that out of the first nineteen letters in Augustine's correspondence, as we have them arranged today, all but one, that is, eighteen letters are either addressed to schoolmen or take up the problems on which

Augustine was engaged in these educational treatises. One letter comes from Maximus the old heathen head of a High School at Madaura, where Augustine had made his course before he was sent to the University at Carthage. Another is Augustine's answer to Maximus. These two letters are important just as far as they are evidences of school training and mentality in the two men who represent two standards of school work—Maximus the heathen, Augustine the Christian—both interested in the schools of the time.

Ten out of these nineteen letters are written to Nebridius, the schoolman, and intimate friend whom Augustine describes in the Confessions. Two letters are addressed to Augustine by Nebridius. In the first letter of this series addressed to Hermogenian, Augustine takes up the subject of his aim in the *Contra Academicos*. Hermogenian had read these studies, and had written evidently to congratulate Augustine on the qualities of his work. In his answer to this letter of congratulation Augustine tells plainly what he thinks of the old heathen system of teaching generally followed in the schools of the time. His censure of the old system logically carries with it the reason for his work on a new method and a new approach to right thinking in the schools. The whole text of the *Contra Academicos* is, as I understand it, the clearest evidence of Augustine's plan to trace the errors of the old systems to their source, to correct the wrong thinking of the time by a standard that is objective, universal, the same for all, and right. Augustine saw, as we see today, I believe, that the accumulating of theories in school work, the habit of centering on selective courses, which is not less old though we are told that it is new, must result eventually in secondhand thinking, in economic and intellectual waste.

Writing to Hermogenian Augustine says: "When at this present time we see no philosophers, excepting perhaps, those who wear the outer dress of philosophers, whom I judge to be unworthy of that honored name, it seems to me that men ought to be brought back into the secure hope of finding truth—men (I repeat) are to be brought back, whom the conclusions of the skeptics, by their choice of words, have frightened, deterred from the (natural) understanding of things. As a consequence, that which was adapted for the time to eliminate the deepest errors (by the skeptics) now is become an impediment for the implanting (that is), the imparting of knowledge." [2]

Further on in this same letter Augustine explains how this system of academic skepticism, which was meant originally to be a safeguard against sophistry and other forms of error, was turned to a wrong use. Second-rate followers of the academic thinkers had mistaken what was meant to be a starting point only and a method of thinking. They had made it the rule and the measure of the whole process of reasoning on the evidences of objective facts and truth. It was entertaining, no doubt, and an easy way for teachers and professors to require the members of the student body, or of a class to prove (if they could) that they were not asleep, or that they were not one and identical with the things that are perceived by the senses, or one with the problems which the mind works out in the science of logic or of mathematics. It was entertaining, perhaps sometimes amusing, but such entertainment and the neglect of first principles were fatal to school work and education.

Augustine knew this by twelve years of experience. He saw the need of what we would call a renewing of the spirit in the schools of the time. It may be presumptuous on my part, but I believe, and I am prepared to hold that this was Augustine's aim during these first months of actual contact with the Faith, and during the years of his monastic community life at Tagaste before he took up the burdens and the duties of the priesthood. It is the plan of life and of work that is evident, and that, I think, is realized in the written works of the time.

The deposit of Faith was secure. Right thinking on the

---

[2] "Hoc autem sæculo, cum iam nullos videamus philosophos, nisi forte amiculo corporis, quos quidem haud censuerim dignos tam venerabili nomine, reducendi mihi videntur homines (si quos Academicorum, per verborum ingenium a rerum comprehensione deterruit sententia) in spem reperiendæ veritatis: Ne id quod, eradicandis altissimis erroribus pro tempore accommodatum fuit, iam incipiat inserendæ scientiæ impedimento esse."

truths of the Creed was taken care of by contemporary teachers and the witnesses of Apostolic Tradition.

These preliminary principles of right reasoning and normal thinking were in peril. The fundamentals of logic, the laws of thought as we teach them in our Catholic school courses today, were being perverted and prostituted to the purposes or to the lack of legitimate purpose in the sophistry and agnosticism of the schools. Here was work to be done that called for the genius and the experience of Augustine as a teacher and a schoolman.

I shall quote briefly from the treatises, which I choose to call Augustine's *textbooks*. A few examples ought to be enough to show the quality of the work that Augustine was doing for education. These quotations, the very words of Augustine, will serve also to reaffirm the fact that Augustine had a plan. They are integral parts of that plan to build education, the school work of the time on the solid foundation of right and sane thinking.

Logically Augustine's work of building up or rebuilding begins with the relations of the normal human mind to the evidences of facts as they come to the senses and the evidence of objective truth as the mind sees it. His work begins with what we call now the *laws of thought* and the *fundamentals of epistemology*.

The words which I quote here are one short argument from the third book *Contra Academicos*.

"How do you know" (this is the objective of the skeptics) "that this material world exists, if the senses are (sometimes) deceived?" Augustine answers: "Your arguments have never had the force to disprove the normal power of the senses so as to show us that *nothing* is perceived—this you have never dared to attempt. You insist, then, vigorously that the world of sense may be other than it appears to be. My answer is that to this whole universe, whatever its quality may be, the world which holds and supports us, the same, I say, which appears to my eyes, which is perceived by me as occupying earth and sky—to this same I give the name *world*. If you, then, say that nothing is perceived by me I will not be in error. He is in error who unreasonably proves that which is perceived by him. If you say that what is seen may be unreal to those who see it, you do not say that nothing is seen. Indeed, if we, not only know nothing, but if nothing at all is perceived by us, then all the cause for dispute (where it is your delight to display your powers) is removed. But if you say that that which is seen by me is not the material world, then you are making a controversy about the name of the thing because I said that by me it is *called* the material world.

"Even, you ask, if you are asleep, is this the world that you see? I have said before that I *call* the material world whatever such is seen by me. But, if you will have it that we *call* the world that only which is seen by those who are wide awake or by those who are sound in mind, then prove, if you can, that the world is not the object of a delusion or of a dream in those who are not in their right mind or who are dreaming. I therefore say this, that all this bulk and structure of bodies (material things) in which we live, whether we are sleeping or waking, whether we are sane of mind or insane—all this bulk, I repeat, is either one or it is not one. Prove (if you can) how that sentence can be untrue. For, if I am asleep, it may be that I have said nothing; or, even if the words have been expressed in sleep, as is not unusual, then it can be that I have spoken not sitting here, not before this audience. But this sentence—the bulk of the world is either one or it is not one—cannot be true. This I affirm, therefore, that I do perceive; I perceive it, and not because I am awake. You may answer that this might have so appeared to me even if I were dreaming, that therefore it comes very near to being untrue. But if it is clear that one world and six worlds are seven worlds it is clear also how I am affected by this objective evidence; and that, I insist, *I know*."

The textbooks in Christian philosophy since the time of Augustine have given us a great variety of forms to prove the skeptics wrong. The sum of their proofs still rests upon what Augustine says here that he *knows*—what we all *know*—the objective relation of facts, of being, of truth—the relation of this objectivity to the human mind.

The point on which I think we ought to insist here is to make

Augustine's way of thinking our own. That way will not be too hard for our students.

It will not be old or antiquated, it will not be new, it will be just our own. The laws of human thought, the relations of the human mind to the evidence of facts, the evidence of truth in concrete form have not changed, they will not change, because they cannot change. We are men made to the image of God, in mind and will, and the image of God does not change or vary with the moods and tenses or the attitudes of men to the objective world. The world and the meaning of the world are still the object of our study, the object of human learning, the object of our teaching, as they were in the fourth century when Augustine, the first Christian schoolman, taught the right way to think about them.

In the field of philosophy and fundamental thinking new theories and new modes have come into vogue. They have had their seasons of fair repute, they have had their followers, many: and they and their following have passed out of fashion. We, of course, cannot afford to neglect these theories, we may not be indifferent to them, as they stand, material facts in the history of human thinking, or, if you will so call it, the history of philosophy. What I would ask you to keep in mind here is this: these accumulated theories, any one of them or all of them have not made another way of right thinking, or of ordering life according to right thought. They have not shown an approach to knowledge and the use of knowledge in forms of applied science other or better than the approach shown by Augustine in the fourth century.

I shall quote here again the words of Augustine in *De Quantitate Animæ* and ask you to ponder, to weigh what he says, to apply his counsel to the methods of teaching philosophy in our Universities today outside the Church.

"Our search," Augustine says to Evodius, "is not for a little thing, not for something that is discovered offhand. We want to know this subject distinctly, if it can be done, and hold on to it. For it is one thing to trust to the authority of others, quite another thing to trust to our own reason (reasonings)."

"To trust authority is a great abridgement, and no labor; which, if you find delight in it, you may read many things that great and good men have said on these subjects"—(You may find them in some way summarized [I would say] in the *Story of Philosophy* by Will Durant, or in the books of John Dewey)— "But if you are to reach the truth by reason" (Augustine continues), "then you must endure many and long ways around, so that no reason may lead you but that alone which is to be called reason, that is, right reason: and not right reason alone, but sure and free from all likeness of falsehood, if in any way this can be found by man, so that no false arguments, or apparent reasonings may betray you."—*De Quanitate Animæ*—Chapter VII.

Our problems, particularly, in the training of men for the priesthood and religious life are, I acknowledge, many and varied. In their bearing on points of practice in civil and political and social life and their relation to advancements of science in the physical world they are constantly changing. But, in kind, these problems are not different from the problems of right thinking in the time of Augustine. The great need of the time, whether we consider time in the environment of our own days, or in the conditions of the fourth century and the fifth—the great need, I repeat, is right thinking and right living according to an objective standard. A safe guide and the proved exponent of that standard is Augustine.

We, in our work, may have to come into contact with systems of thought and educational habits of mind that do not square with the Christian and Catholic principles of Augustine. We have this advantage over the non-Catholic and neutral schools and universities—Augustine is our sure guide. As the ideal teacher, his *Philosophy,* his *system of thinking* on the meaning of life is safe.

Our position as Catholic Schoolmen at the present time is not unlike the position of Saint Augustine in the first Augustinian Study House at Tagaste or in the retreat at *Cassiago.* The changes, which we note, in forms of civil government, in our social and economic life are very real and far-reaching; but they are accidental changes only. They have introduced no difference that is substantial in the normal life and powers and operations of the human mind. The material facts of our life on this earth, the right understanding and the meaning of those facts are still expressed literally and well in the old forms of Augustine's reasoning and his definitions.

On this point I shall cite here and quote the words contained in a personal letter written by a teacher in one of our western diocesan seminaries. This professor had received, by request, a copy of Saint Augustine's *"De Magistro"* translated into English. In acknowledgment some time later, under date of June 6, 1934, he writes—I quote: "I loaned the book to a professor of Education in the University of Washington (the State of Washington). He has made good use of it; and it has opened his eyes to what the Church Fathers knew about *Education* long before the days of John Dewey *et al.*" [3]

I recognize and confess that the objection may be made that what I have said here has been said from one side of our problems only—from the side which contemplates Augustine as a genius in the work of education in the distant past.

It may be said that we venerate him as a master mind, but that we can hardly be expected to take his work into our courses in the Arts and Philosophy. To such an objection I would answer that it begs the question. As true Augustinians we may hardly have the thought of studying Augustine's principles to the exclusion of the more modern scholastic system and forms in philosophy —but, where these principles of Augustine are fundamental to the newer ways and methods, we ought to know them, study them, and make them our own. This is work, which, I think, ought to give character and quality to our Augustinian training schools. There is room here for opportunity and for the future, for our best students and teachers, to find, to point out and to show just where Augustine laid foundations for the later scholastic forms of the classical Middle Age, where he did pioneer work for right thinking and sound teaching in modern education.

---

[3] From the Rev. Joseph P. Dougherty, St. Edward's Seminary, Kenmore University Station, Seattle, Washington.

# SAINT AUGUSTINE AND EDUCATION

THE rigid requirements of present-day State-directed teacher-training afford no incentive, and leave little time, for the study and mastery of methods and technique other than those prescribed by the State. For that reason, we refrain from entering into a minute discussion or detailed exposition of our holy Founder's unique method of educating, however sound, simple, natural and efficient that method may be. Our present-day teachers must be credited and equipped in conformity with the State standards to which we have referred; and those standards have been elaborated and determined with no explicit reference to Augustine, and with no thought of his indirect influence on present-day educational methods. But we are firm in the conviction that even a brief résumé of our holy Founder's marvelous accomplishments will inevitably improve us as teachers by arousing in us an impelling enthusiasm and by instilling into us a sustaining confidence. We imbibe the glowing enthusiasm which his personality never fails to impart, and we acquire the salutary confidence which his unrivaled proficiency must inevitably afford. Realizing that his great accomplishments are due, not to genius alone but to industry as well, we acquire a helpful confidence in our own power of proficiency; for we can, at least, emulate him in assiduity, although we can never hope to approach him in genius.

In the words of Tixeront, "Saint Augustine is, incontestably, the greatest Doctor that the Church has ever had." [1] And, according to Windelband, Saint Augustine "is the real teacher of the Middle Ages." [2] His genius was universal, and his toil was unremitting. Prodigious genius and constant assiduity combined to produce the universal teacher of succeeding generations. His dominant and pervading influence on medieval, modern and present-day schools of thought has been profoundly grasped and forcibly expressed by the foremost scholars of today. By

[1] *Histoire des dogmes*, ed. 7, 1924, Vol. II, p. 354.
[2] *Lehrbuch der Geschichte der Philosophie*, ed. 5, 1910, p. 220.

none perhaps, has this signal service, in its twofold aspect, been rendered so extensively and incisively as by the erudite and judicious author, Bernhard Jansen, S.J. In regard to Augustine's ideas and character, Doctor Jansen is both luminous in exposition and sympathetic in delineation. By frequent quotation, and more frequent paraphrase, from the pages of Jansen and others, as well as by comments of our own, we shall endeavor to present to our readers the Augustine who has been "the real teacher of the Middle Ages," and who, in our own day, has become the compelling cynosure of astonished eyes.

In the field of exegesis, he is a towering figure, still clearly discernible through the lengthening vista of the centuries from the twentieth to the fifth. Contemporary of Ambrose and Jerome, he easily surpasses them, as well as all others, in venturesome originality and in profound speculation on the Biblical account of creation.[3] His catechetical contributions, intended as apt nourishment for the adolescent Church of his day, have continued to supply delicious food and suitable sustenance for the Church grown to maturity. His homilies, characterized by sublimity and exactitude, vivid imagination and vast erudition, clear exposition and forceful appeal, have, without interruption, afforded models and material for sacred orators in every succeeding age: they occupy a pre-eminent place in the Roman Breviary. In mysticism and asceticism, his writings form the reservoir which "fed richly for a thousand years the piety and the preaching of priest and monk and saint, the devotional life of whole peoples, their ideas of holiness, and the institutions through which it expressed itself."[4] Philosophy of History and, in Christian times, History of Philosophy, date back to the author of genius who composed the immortal *City of God*—a work in which Augustine marshals all the divers transactions of universal history, describes various customs, beliefs, and forms of worship; and then, at once with the inventive stroke of marvelous genius and the moving force of self-evident truth, summarizes the lesson of history with the

[3] *Cf.* Zahm, *Bible, Science and the Faith,* 1895, pp. 70 et seq.
[4] Shahan, *The Catholic World,* 1930, p. 580.

striking aphorism: "Two loves have formed two kingdoms." In a sublime strain of elevated sentiment and lofty expression, he portrays the establishment, the constitution, and the government of the two kingdoms founded on love—the Kingdom of Good and the Kingdom of Evil. The former arises from the love of God; the latter, from the love of self. "Heavenly love," he says, "is the love of God even unto contempt of self. Earthly love, on the other hand, is love of self even unto contempt of God." [5] Never before or since has the teaching of history been grasped so profoundly or so succinctly expressed.

In theology, Augustine's pre-eminence has never been questioned, doubted or ignored. On the contrary, it has been universally recognized and constantly proclaimed. Saint Albert the Great decided that "in questions of faith or morals, it is impious to contradict Saint Augustine." [6] And the distinguished Thomist, Cardinal Zigliara, testifies to "the homage rendered him by all the votaries of theology and philosophy, especially by that most refulgent star, Saint Thomas of Aquin, who has perhaps equaled him in splendor." [7] Theologians have without cessation enriched their minds and illumined their pages with the profound reasonings and daring speculations of his monumental theological productions. The Church has set the indelible seal of her infallible magisterium on much of the teaching of the Doctor of Grace. "Augustine is the creative intuitionist. He is the first to think the difficult and daring thoughts which none of the profound and sublime philosophers of the entire Greek philosophy had surmised—the notion of creation as a *productio ex nihilo sui et subjecti.* . . . He surpassed all the profound speculations of the great Cappadocians and the other Greek and Latin Fathers, concerning the issue of the LOGOS from the Father. . . . He is the fundamental theological teacher of the doctrine of grace." [8]

Catholic philosophy must look to Augustine as the integrator of Christian Revelation with whatever was true in pagan specula-

---

[5] *De civitate Dei, lib.* XIV, cap. 28.
[6] *Summa theol.,* pars 2, tr. 14, qu. 184.
[7] *Della luce intellettuale,* 1847, Vol. I, cap. 8.
[8] Jansen, *Miscellanea Augustiniana, Utrecht,* 1930, p. 209.

tion. Living in the fifth century, educated in pagan schools and permeated with pagan influences, he sought happiness in the pursuit of truth; and he pursued truth through the various schools of pagan philosophy. For him, therefore, the various philosophic systems were no mere academic theories: they were practical rules of life. He appraised them; and, when he accepted them, he assimilated and lived them. And when he rejected them, he was able to retain the particles of truth which they contained. For, as Augustine himself affirms, "there is no doctrine so false as to contain no truth." [9] "Henceforth the heart of the youthful Augustine holds a fixed and definite course. Now truth will be for him the sole preoccupation, the sole aim of his desire, the sole object of his love. . . . In search of truth, Augustine exhausts the circle of the philosophic schools, passing eagerly from sect to sect, from error to error, from descent to descent. . . . At length, after much effort, fatigue, and disillusion, he descries a ray of light in Platonism. Soon afterwards, his noble perseverance receives a just recompense and a crowning reward. He discovers, in Christianity, truth in its integrity—truth pure and undefiled." [10] And, finding truth, he found happiness, because, in truth, he found God. "Where I found the truth, there I found my God, who is the Truth itself." [11] "A happy life is joy in the truth. For this is joy in Thee, who art the Truth, O God, my light." [12]

Having embraced Christianity—having found truth and happiness—he returned to his native Tagaste, where, living in community with brethren, he devoted his time to prayer and fasting and the writing of books. Contrary to his wish, but not against his will, his status is soon changed from that of layman to cleric, and the scene of his labors is transferred from Tagaste to Hippo; but for the rest of his life he lived in community, and devoted himself to prayer and fasting and the writing of books. In the writing of books, no less than in prayer and fasting, his motive is a supernatural one: he will strive to bring all men to a knowl-

[9] *Quaest. evangel.*, lib. II, qu. 40.
[10] Vega, *St. Augustine*, 1931, p. 173.
[11] *Confess.*, lib. X., cap. 24.
[12] *Confess.*, lib. X., cap. 23.

edge of the truth, to a knowledge of "God, who is the Truth."
And, in pursuance of this aim, he will guard them against error
—error which keeps men "far from God." His previous training and his present aim are indelibly impressed upon all his
future writings. He drew copiously from pagan streams, but he
purified the flow through the filter of Christian Revelation.
"Augustine assimilated all the currents of preceding ages, and
all the influence of his own day. He fused them in the crucible
of his intellect, and formed them into a new and more powerful
synthesis. Though developed in an environment essentially
Latin, his native growth was copiously irrigated and abundantly
nourished by various Greek and Oriental currents. Of Christianity and primitive Platonism, he elaborated a synthesis in
which, by virtue of his originality, the Christian element pre-
dominates. His synthesis, however contested and however
contestable, has successfully dominated the Western Church
throughout all its history." [13]   In the elaboration of his synthesis, our holy Founder evinces a special predilection for Platonism, but he by no means ignores the other pagan schools. He
finds precious grains of truth commingled with error in all of
them. All these grains of truth are weighed in the balance with
Christian Revelation. "In the intellectual realm, Saint Augustine
is, then, at once the repository of ancient achievement and the
initiator of modern development—in a word, the bond between
Pagan culture and Christian thought." [14]   In the beginning, his
decided predilection for Platonism leads him to overestimate its
merits; but his reverent and profound study of the Sacred Scripture soon moderates his glowing enthusiasm, and gradually dis-
pels his consequent errors, in this regard. His efforts to reconcile
Platonism with Christianity resulted in failure; but that partial
failure occasioned a noted success—the cleansing of the dross
of error from the ore of truth in Pagan speculation, and the
consequent welding of a Christian philosophy. "Platonic philosophy and Johannine theology—these Augustine welded into a

[13] Eucken, *Die Lebensanschauungen der Grossen Denker,* 1919, p. 240.
[14] Vega, *op. cit.,* p. 75.

vigorous, unified system, fusing them into one permanent, homogeneous whole. This is his creative masterpiece—the greatest stroke of genius in his entire philosophy. In consequence of this perfect reconciliation of philosophy and theology—of reason and faith, the Doctor of Hippo exercised a profound influence, as fundamental as inspiring, upon the entire series of Medieval thinkers, and, above all, upon that incarnation of the speculative spirit, the Angelic Doctor. Through the instrumentality of these disciples, our Supreme Patristic has become the peerless teacher of the Scholastic and all subsequent Christian thinkers—an ever-vital teacher, combining the eternal freshness of youth with the immortal wisdom of age." [15]

In his *Confessions,* "the greatest spiritual autobiography ever written by a man," Augustine reveals his soul as the soul of no other saint or sage was ever revealed. At once intimate as a soliloquy and detached as scientific research, his thrilling *Confiteor* records and analyzes "every phase of his soul's experience and reveals every secret of the *penetralia mentis*—those psychic impressions, perturbations, agitations, crises, ordeals, depressions, exaltations, dubitations, and satisfactions. . . . In Augustine's philosophy, the strongest and most fascinating feature is the harmonious union of subjective, personal traits with objective, impersonal reality." [16] In all his writings, Augustine at once humanizes and spiritualizes whatever he touches. Hence his universal appeal, and hence his inevitable leading to God. "A star of the first magnitude, he traverses the empyrean, trailing in his wake the vivid light of living truth. Neither Socrates, nor Plato, nor Aristotle, nor any of the great philosophers of Antiquity, has ever spoken a language like his. With them, however great, one always stands on the earth in converse with men. With Augustine, we feel that we stand upon Sinai or Tabor in communion with God. Who has ever written books that surpass Augustine's *City of God, Genesis,* or *Trinity?* Who has not meditated in tears as he read Augustine's *Confessions?* In that

[15] Jansen, *Wege der Weltweisheit,* 1924, p. 85.
[16] Jansen, *Wege der Weltweisheit,* 1924, p. 70.

book, he speaks as no man ever spoke before, or will, we fear, ever speak again." [17]

Regarding Augustine's doctrines, however, one must always bear in mind that their author wrote as occasion demanded and opportunity offered. While yet a catechumen, he began to write; and as an aged Bishop, he continued to compose. Throughout the busy intervening years, he wrote by progressing, and he progressed by writing. And in the progress of his writing, he learned to detect various errors which had at first escaped him. Hence the marked difference in philosophic outlook and criterion between his early *Dialogues* and his *Retractations*—those "pitilessly severe, critical revisions of his entire literary output." Truly, those *Retractations* are the most beautiful and eloquent expression of his keen, brilliant, vigorous intellect and of his noble, honest, and humble soul." [18]

His pages are inspirited with the soul of his own ardent longing; and his longing is for knowledge of God, and self-knowledge. *Noverim me. noverim Te.*[19]  His earnest petition for this twofold salutary and satisfying knowledge was granted in such generous measure that, when discoursing on God, his lips, like the prophet's lips, are touched with fire; and when writing of self, his pen is dipped in his own heart's life-blood. He lives in his pages as vividly as the chief character in a drama; and his life is the drama that depicts the struggles, the tortures, the vacillations, the failures, and the ultimate triumph of an earth-fettered soul seeking heavenward flight. From sheerest depths he rose to loftiest heights of moral greatness. All up that rugged acclivity —that more than Alpine steep—he had to work his way as well against the innate propensities of fallen nature as against the atmospheric contagion of a dissolute age. All up that toilsome ascent, he walked on naked, bleeding feet; and on aching shoulders he had to carry his heavy load of youth's sad errors. In long and devious windings, his journey led him through the

[17] Zigliara, *op. cit., ibid.*
[18] Jansen, *Wege, usw.,* p. 71.
[19] *Soliloquia,* lib., II, cap. 1.

dark night of error and through the misty clouds of doubt; but he gained the peaceful summit, illumined and warmed by the vitalizing sun of radiant truth. On this mountain summit of intellectual and moral greatness, his writings formed that reservoir which "fed richly for a thousand years the piety and the preaching of priest and monk and saint, the devotional life of whole peoples, their ideas of holiness, and the institutions through which it expressed itself."

Augustine's writings not only fed the piety and the preaching of priest and monk and saint, but fashioned their philosophy as well. "From Augustine's own day in the fifth century to the days of Saint Thomas of Aquin in the thirteenth, the greatest philosophers and theologians adhere to the school of Augustine." [20] "It is incredible to what extent this genius, so rich and so cultivated, has furnished ideas and theories to all the Doctors of the Middle Ages. Before we attribute to any of them the discovery of a new system, we should examine the works of that holy Father, in order to ascertain whether the so-called new system is not found already explained in his writings." [21]

In modern times, however, his purely philosophical works became an almost uncultivated field—at first neglected, then forgotten, and, finally, almost totally unknown. The cardinal influence of the Christian Plato on subsequent metaphysics—an influence at once dominant, pervading and universal—escaped the discernment of pre-Hegelian historians of thought. In his purely philosophical works, the patent metaphysics was unrecognized; for the works themselves were disregarded. His *Confessions*, the *Trinity*, and the *City of God* retained their popularity and resplendent celebrity; yet, in those works, the latent metaphysics, the incidental philosophy, was but obscurely perceived and dimly discerned. The Renaissance and the Religious Revolt largely furnished the occasion for this obscuration of Augustine's philosophy. In matters of faith and theology, they gladly consulted the Church Fathers. In matters of sheer philosophy, they returned for masters and models almost exclusively to Classical Antiquity. They derided Scholasticism—the philosophy of the Middle Ages—and represented it as a retrogressive movement, a sterile, one-sided revival of an exploded Aristotelianism. Catholic philosophers defended that which was specifically attacked—Medieval Scholasticism. Medieval Scholastics, having thus become the chief object of attack and defense, came to be regarded as, not only the systematizers and expositors of Catholic philosophy, but its initiators as well. Thus it happened that, while the name of the Bishop of Hippo has always loomed large in the pages of theological writings, it almost disappeared from current philosophy.

But, with the birth of the Historical Sense, the Medieval philosophical system was rediscovered and made manifest. Discoveries as genuine as wonderful, illuminated and astonished the naïve modern mind. In contradistinction to the adverse criticisms of the Renaissance and the Reformation, Scholastic philosophy was shown to be no mere mental treadmill for artificial, mechanical, monotonous intellectual gymnastics. Neither was it that stagnant pool of stale opinions which unenlightened or hostile critics had falsely represented it to be. Scholasticism was a flourishing intellectual realm through whose fair domain flowed the noble river of thought which derived its main current from Aristotle's perennial source. With this chief stream there commingled divers tributaries of Platonic-Augustinian origin, as well as limpid streams from crystal springs that rose within the boundaries of Scholasticism's own domain. All these imparted to the system a healthful motion, an interesting diversity, a pleasing variety. Over this flourishing realm ruled Saint Thomas Aquinas, Prince of Scholasticism, worthy successor of peerless rulers, legitimate heir to the harmoniously united kingdoms of Aristotle and Augustine.

The discovery of Augustine's influence on early Scholasticism led to a direct study of Augustine's philosophy. And the direct study of Augustine's philosophy led to most interesting and instructive discoveries. Philosophical methods parading as modern discoveries were found described and utilized in Augustine's writings. Descartes' *Cogito, ergo sum* had been hailed as a brilliant stroke of inventive genius, and its author had been universally styled as the "Father of Modern Philosophy." Yet, twelve centuries earlier, Augustine had employed the same method in the solution of the same problem, and had enunciated the same thought, when he said *"Si fallor, sum."* [22] From the seventeenth century down to our own day, the chief non-Scholastic philosophic systems—Rationalism, Empiricism, Criticism, Historicism—exhaust themselves on questions of epistemology, and strain themselves to emphasize their agreement with, or their divergence from, the Cartesian method and the Cartesian inference, *Cogito, ergo sum.* Except in isolated instances, which constitute happy exceptions, you will search in vain for any reference to the great Patristic's conclusive refutation of Scepticism with the cogent and irrefutable *argumentum ad hominem, Si fallor, sum.* The name of Augustine had almost disappeared from current philosophy.

Antiquity, as a rule, concerned itself but little with the problem of reflex certitude—a problem which pervades and perplexes Modern Philosophy. The exigencies of his day did not demand of Augustine the exposition and solution of that perplexing problem. But, just as the Father of Christian Philosophy, with the anticipation of a born metaphysical genius, had stated and solved the problem of direct certitude centuries before Descartes; so, of reflex certitude, had he, in large measure, a presentiment of the difficulties—difficulties whose very formulation has made famous the name of Immanuel Kant.

Augustine's psychology—his introspective method, his just observation, his keen analysis, and his vivid description of psychic phenomena—makes him the admired of present-day psychological schools. His theories on cosmogony and evolution, antedating modern theories on those subjects by thirteen hundred years, were found to contain observations, orientations, hypotheses, and methods of approach which heretofore had been almost uni-

[22] *De civ. Dei*, lib. XI, cap. 26.

versally regarded—except by theologians—as of recent origin and development. Most astonishing of all, perhaps, was the vast profusion of precious pedagogical principles and precepts found, either neatly arranged in orderly sequence or promiscuously scattered with other material, in nearly all his writings. At times, the maxims of pedagogy are enumerated with the utmost precision, and urged with the finest art of persuasion. At all times, however, Augustine is the introspective psychologist who understands the workings of the human mind, and who knows how to explore its inmost recesses—to analyze the processes of learning, remembering, forgetting, and recognizing. His pedagogical method, formulated and employed in the fifth century, is at once ancient and modern—ancient in its discovery, and, in its rediscovery, modern. Our neoteric advocates of advanced methods in pedagogy may well study Augustine with profit to themselves and with consequent enrichment of educational psychology.

Many another topic of present-day perplexing concern was found sketched or expounded in his multifarious productions. A most striking instance of his present-day timeliness is furnished by the fact that today scholars are diligently consulting his works with the aim of discovering his views on the burning question of *sanctions against an aggressor nation.* "On the question of 'sanctions,' as they are understood at the moment, Saint Augustine is perhaps not quite so explicit. . . . But still the principle of sanctions is clearly taught in the *De civitate Dei.* . . . What Augustine saw so clearly fifteen hundred years ago, Europe is blindly groping towards today. . . . There is a gleam of light which may be the end of the tunnel—and when we have stumbled our way to the end we may find that we have been travelling *backwards* to Augustine from whence Europe started her great and glorious adventure fifteen centuries ago." [23] No wonder that modern scholars proclaim him modern, and rapturously exclaim: "He belongs to us, he is ours." [24] Harnack has called him "the foremost modern man." [25]

[23] Wadsworth, *The Clergy Review,* 1936, pp. 28, 29, 30.
[24] Jansen, *Wege, usw.,* p. 73.
[25] Seeberg, *Lehrbuch der Dogmengeschichte,* 1910, Vol. II, p. 358.

Before we commit ourselves to unqualified approval of that dubious honor to Augustine's fame, let us hear the just appraisal of Augustine's modernity, as formulated by that profound and discriminating student of Augustine's doctrines, Bernhard Jansen, S.J.

> "A modern thinker" I have called Augustine. "Up-to-date" I should term his thoughts. . . . To describe them adequately and exhaustively, I would characterize them as "up-to-date" and, at the same time, "unfashionable"—in a word, "universal": so universal, that they must inevitably include modernity; so universal, that they cannot pass away with the passing fashion. His epistemology is modern in its methods, but unmodern in its results; modern in its basis, but unmodern in its culmination; modern in its human feeling, but unmodern in its spiritual achievement. Like the modern mode, it proceeds from the data of consciousness; but, unlike the modern mode, it leads to absolute, eternal criteria. His psychology is modern in the patient observation and keen analysis of its fundamental empiricism; but unmodern in the comprehensive speculation of its metaphysical superstructure. . . . Modern is the evolution of all later life from primitive, simultaneously established seminal powers; unmodern, the constancy and sharp delimitation of distinct species. Most especially modern is his introspection, his fondness for the study of the inner life; unmodern, his prospection, his linking of the world of consciousness and ideality with the world of absolute, eternal, divine reality.[26]

* * *

We have given but a faint and very inadequate outline of the accomplishments of Augustine, the genius. In order to come closer to rendering justice to our subject, and satisfaction to our readers, we have confined ourselves almost exclusively to quotations or paraphrases from authoritative sources; and have, as far as possible, refrained from inserting comments of our own. In the process of selection, we have suffered, not from a dearth of material, but from a superabundance. For, down through the ages, he has shone like a refulgent star for the coldly intel-

[26] Jansen, *Wege, usw.*, p. 79.

lectual, and like a vitalizing sun for the warmly emotional and religious. In the words of the illustrious Villemain:—"In whatever epoch he be considered, in whatever circumstances he be placed, it appears that his genius could not shine with greater lustre, or be more responsive or universal; mysticism and asceticism, poesy and eloquence, arts and science, history and apologetics, morals and Scripture, philosophy and theology—he studies them all, he treats of them all, and he masters them all. With the same facility and competency, he treats of music and of free will; and with the same facility and competency, he explains the psychologic phenomena of memory and reasons on the decadence of the Roman Empire." [27]

And if, at times, the light of this refulgent star grew dim, or the warmth of this radiant sun was dissipated, the dimming and the dissipating were due to the interposition of passing clouds—clouds that rose from religious rancor or intellectual aberrations. Today, his fame has pierced the clouds, and his noble figure is once again revealed. The modern world merely deigned a glance, and was charmed to behold. And beholding, listened; and listening, heard the voice from Antiquity, and recognized the tone of Modernity. Today his words are being rendered by a hundred translators, his doctrines are being interpreted by a thousand commentators, and his ideas are avidly devoured as the mental nurture of a million readers. Augustine, the voice from Antiquity, is, by the anticipation of genius, rich with universal wisdom, and full of modern appeal. To paraphrase Jansen, Augustine is unmodernly modern. He at once corroborates the modern spirit, and corrects it. Fifteen hundred years ago, in the midst of Ancient Paganism, his age was inundated with many of the issues of Modern Paganism. From some of those, he drained the source; of others, he diverted the current to the Christian stream. Universal genius, he has been contemporary of every age: he is of kindred spirit with our own. And our own age joins the swelling chorus of his praise, and calls him Great.

[27] *Tableau de l'éloquence chretienne*, 1853, p. 363.

Having, to the best of our ability, and within the limits of the space allowed us, "outlined the achievements and merits of a man with whom—on account of the vigor of his acute genius, on account of the richness and the elevation of his doctrine, on account of his sanctity elevated to such heights, on account of his invincible defense of Catholic truth—you could compare scarcely any, or at most a few of those who have attained distinction from the beginning of the human race even to the present day," [28] let us now, again to the best of our ability, briefly trace the genesis and development of that towering personality, "that paragon of intellect and industry, whose productions astonish by their number, dazzle by their brilliancy, enamor by their feeling, and instruct by the erudition they contain." [29] In pursuance of this aim, we cannot avoid a few biographical references; but our chief purpose will be the revealment of his character-formation. As a boy, he attended school in his native town of Tagaste, and, later, at Madaura. Without doubt, nature had endowed him with unusual talent; and his proficiency at studies was such as to justify the hope of a learned career for the son of Patrick and Monica. Later, he enrolled at a higher school in Carthage; and, as a result of his talents and attainments, he became a professor of rhetoric. This career he pursued—first at Carthage, later at Rome, and finally in Milan—until his conversion to Christianity, in the thirty-third year of his age. During those years, what was the motive that impelled him, and what was the hope that sustained him in the career which he had embraced? We need not conjecture: he has plainly confessed them. They were his need of money, his desire for fame and his disinterested predilection for teaching. "During those years, I taught the art of rhetoric; and, being myself overcome by a desire of gain, I made sale of loquacity which might overcome others." [30] "I conceived it to be a matter of much importance to me, if my words and my learning might be pub-

---

[28] Pius XI, Encycl., *Ad salutem,* April, 1930.

[29] Vega, *op. cit.,* p. 20.

[30] *Confess.,* lib. IV, cap. 2.

lished in the ears of that great man, that if he should approve
them I might be the more set on fire, while, if he should dis-
esteem them, this vain heart of mine would have been deeply
wounded." [31] "I did not therefore dispose myself to go to Rome
because more gain or greater honor was promised me—though
these things also wrought somewhat then upon me—but this was
the chief and almost the only cause, that I had heard how there
the young men used to study more quietly and were subject to
better discipline." [32]  Seeking to advance himself, he migrated to
Rome; and, seeking further advance, he obtained a professor-
ship at Milan. Judging by his qualities of mind, as revealed in
his later works, we may well surmise that he was undoubtedly a
brilliant professor. But history is silent regarding any fame
that he may have acquired during those weary years in which
he so earnestly sought it. And as to his wealth, it probably was
not sufficient to afford him a suitable residence. At any rate, it
was, not to his own villa, but to that of a friend, that he retired
to seek solitude for contemplation. While he sought happiness
in wealth and glory, he acquired neither wealth nor glory—nor
happiness. During those weary years, at once so void of happiness and so full of anxiety—weary years spent "far from
God" [33]—he wrote not a single syllable that has come down to
posterity.

Embracing Christianity, he renounced all worldly longing, and
surrendered himself unreservedly to God. He now resolves to
utilize his talents, not for wealth or self-aggrandizement, not for
fame or human vanity, but for God's eternal honor, and his
neighbor's spiritual welfare. From Milan, he returns to Tagaste,
where, "seeking neither wealth nor worldly honors, . . . he lived
for God, in community with disciples, in prayer, fasting and good
works, . . . teaching both at home and abroad by oral and written
discourses." [34]  He prays, in thanksgiving for the supernatural
grace bestowed on him—bestowed so signally as to be compared

[31] *Confess.*, lib. IV, cap. 14.
[32] *Confess.*, lib. V, cap. 8.
[33] *Cf. Confess.*, lib. III, cap. 6, n. 11.
[34] Possidius, *Vita Augustini*, cc. 2, 3.

to the divine enlightenment of Saint Paul on the road to Damascus. He writes books, in order to instruct others, and to guard their lives against the pitfalls that had beset his own. The books that he wrote have lived: they have instructed and inspired succeeding generations; they have made his name immortal and his fame secure. Those books were written for God; they were written while their author spent his busy days with disciples, in prayer and fasting. They are lovably human, for they were written with friends; they are permeated with the spiritual, for their author composed them while he lived for God. Prayer and fasting eroded the carnal fetters which had bound his genius; and the alembic of his genius at once humanizes and spiritualizes whatever he touches. While he consciously sought happiness in fame, he neither acquired fame nor found happiness. When, from a supernatural motive, he eschewed all thought of fame, and sought only God's glory and his neighbor's welfare, he found the happiness which had so long eluded him; and Fame, no longer courted, came unbidden and marked him as her own. "Whosoever will save his life, shall lose it; and whosoever shall lose his life for my sake and the gospel, shall save it." [35]

In the person of Augustine, we find two teachers, the Pagan Professor and the Christian Doctor. The Pagan Professor's impulsion is derived from motives, not sordid or sinful, but merely human. The Christian Doctor, forgetful of self, seeks only the glory of God, his own and his neighbor's salvation. The one seeks happiness in the ephemeral bubble of fame, in the volatile froth of capricious adulation; the other sets his heart where alone the human heart finds rest—in God and the things that pertain to His glory. The one strives for promotion—to Rome and to Milan—because worldly prospects seem auspicious; the other is guided unreservedly by the will of his Superiors. The one strives to be seen by men, and praised by them; the other seeks seclusion, prosecutes his labors "in community with brethren, and devoted to prayer and fasting." The one, as far as we know, never rose above mediocrity; and he lives only in con-

[35] *Marc.*, VIII, 35.

trast with the other, who has become "the greatest Doctor that the Church has ever had,"—the genial Church Father, the Doctor of Grace, the Library of the Church, the Oracle of Christianity, and the chosen preceptor of succeeding generations, —Saint Augustine, whose dynamic personality charges with enthusiasm, and whose salutary example instills into us a sustaining confidence. Which of them should teachers imitate?

# SAINT AUGUSTINE, A FOUNDER OF WESTERN MONASTICISM

THE following notes have been compiled mainly from:

First—The Works of Saint Augustine, chiefly the *Confessions, Letters,* and *Sermons.*

Second—*The Life of Saint Augustine,* by Possidius; that compiled from his works by the Benedictine Fathers, and making Volume 15 of the same; that by an anonymous Augustinian, in the *Biblioteca Agostiniana,* Florence; and that by Father Alfonso Camillo de Romanis.

Third—*The Monasticon Augustinianum,* by Nicholas Crusenius, and the *History of the Origin, etc., of the Various Orders Following Saint Augustine's Rule,* by Albert Le Mire, published in Brussels in 1611.

\* \* \* \* \*

Before his baptism, Augustine already wished to retire from the turmoil of the world. We read in the *Confessions* (VI, 14):

> Many of us friends, consulting on and abhorring the turbulent vexations of human life, had considered and now almost determined upon living at ease and separate from the turmoil of men.

Clearly, this was hardly a religious motive, nor was the group to be considered a religious community. It was to be set up in this manner:

> We were to bring whatever we could severally procure, and make a common household, so that, through the sincerity of our friendship, nothing should belong more to one than to the other; but the whole, being derived from all, should as a whole belong to each, and the whole unto all. It seemed to us that this society might consist of ten persons some of whom were very rich. . . . we had arranged, too, that two officers should be chosen yearly for the providing of all necessary things, whilst the rest were left undisturbed.

(From this we might conclude that the office of Procurator is the oldest in Augustinian ideology.)  But this fair dream vanished when faced with reality.  We read further:

> When we began to reflect whether the wives, which some of us had already, and others hoped to have, would permit this, all that plan which was so well framed, broke to pieces in our hands, and was utterly wrecked.

Thus finished Saint Augustine's first plan for community life.

It was some time after this that Augustine heard for the first time of Christian Monasticism.  He tells in detail (*Conf.*, VIII, 6) of the visit paid to him by a fellow African, an official at the Imperial Court, named Pontitianus.  The conversation turned to:

> Anthony, the Egyptian monk, whose name was in high repute among Christians, though up to that time, not familiar to us.  When he (Pontitianus) came to know this, he lingered on that topic, imparting to us a knowledge of this man so eminent, and marveling at our ignorance. . . . from this his conversation turned to the companies in the monasteries, and their manners so fragrant unto Thee, and of the fruitful deserts of the wilderness of which we knew nothing.  And there was a monastery at Milan, without the walls of the City, full of good brethren under the fostering care of Ambrose, and we were ignorant of it.

Later Augustine paid at least one visit to this retreat, as we read in his *De Moribus Ecclesiæ Catholicæ* (70):

> "I saw," he writes, "at Milan a lodging house of Saints in number not a few, presided over by one priest, a man of great excellence and learning."

Augustine planned to leave Italy after his conversion, together with his son Adeodatus, Monica, his mother, and his friends Alypius and Evodius.  He writes of this plan in the *Confessions* (IX, 8):

> Thou, Who makest men to dwell of one mind in a house did associate with us Evodius also, a young man of our City, who, when serving as an Agent for Public Affairs was

converted unto Thee and baptized prior to us; and relinquishing his secular service, prepared himself for Thine. We were together, and together were we about to dwell with a holy purpose. We sought for some place where we might be most useful in our service to Thee, and were going back together to Africa.

The death of his mother at Ostia during this journey changed his plans, and after her funeral he went back to Rome with his friends. During his stay there he was edified by the life of the monks and the nuns he met in that City. He tells us (*De Mor. Ecc. Cath.*, 70):

At Rome, too, I knew many monasteries (*diversoria*) in which those who were outstanding for gravity, prudence, and sacred learning, governed others who lived joined to them in Christian charity, holiness and freedom.

He goes on to describe their ascetic life, dilates on their fasting and passes on to say:

Nor was this true of men alone

and then describes the nuns' régime.

After this Roman interlude he followed out his original plan, and with his friends, went on to Africa. Possidius in the *Life* (III) says:

It pleased him to return to Africa and his own house and fields accompanied by his friends and townsmen. Arrived there and settled down with those who remained with him, he cast aside worldly cares and for three years he lived with God, fasting and praying, doing good works and meditating day and night on the law of God. And he taught by word and writing to those present and absent, the things God revealed to him during his prayers and meditations.

These first companions were Alypius, Evodius, Novatus, Severus, and the young Adeodatus. This community (shall we call it) was gathered together in a house outside the walls of Tagaste, though not far from the town. It would seem from an expression of Augustine that he had reserved to himself the use of this property when he sold his possessions and distributed the proceeds to the poor. The fruit of the discussions held in this early community are gathered in Augustine's volume entitled *The Eighty-three Questions*. Further fruit of his activity and his meditations in this retreat are the works *De Genesi Contra Manichœos*, *De Musica*, *De Magistro* and *De Vera Religione*. Some of his most instructive and beautiful letters also date from this period of comparative peace.

So sure was Augustine of the value of this religious life that he made various efforts to bring other souls to the haven he had found in this suburban retreat. As a matter of fact, it was precisely during a little trip he had made for the purpose of persuading a minor State official to leave all and join the group, that he was seized by the congregation of the Church of Hippo and induced by pious violence to accept priestly orders.

Thus the three-year retreat ended, and Augustine was forced to change his plan of living as a layman. Ordained a priest, he immediately organized a monastery. Possidius writes in the *Life* (V):

> He (Augustine) soon founded a monastery within the Church; there he began to live with the servants of God according to the manner and rules established under the Holy Apostles; chiefly that no one in that society should have anything of his own, but all should be in common and given to each as each had need; as he himself had done on returning from across the sea to his own Country.

This insistance on common life shows up in many of Augustine's letters. He allowed (*Ep.*, 64) one of his subjects to accept the gift of a field because the products could be put into common use; for himself he refused a gift of fine clothing as unworthy of the poor son of a poor father, and different from the clothing of his brethren; he refused also the offer of a freight boat which an injudicious friend had tried to donate to the monastery, on the grounds that its use would disrupt community life.

From hints and allusions made in various of the genuine works of our Holy Father, we may deduce that he and his brethren at this time wore a dark or black habit with a cowl or hood. *(III ad Pet. 40 De Op. Mon. I Ep. 199.)* Many more details are to be found in the *Sermones ad Fratres in Eremo,* but the critics have relegated these works to the limbo of unskilled fiction.

Augustine was soon made a bishop and then he thought it best to leave the monastery which he had founded. His chief reason seems to have been the calls made on his charity by the obligations of hospitality. He realized that a bishop must meet and entertain many people, and frequently have pilgrims and strangers in his house. Such activity he thought unsuited to the quiet of his monastery, and so he again left his brethren and took up his residence near the cathedral church. But even here he insisted that his priests live with him and practice the common life. Those who refused were allowed to go to other dioceses to exercise their priestly functions. This new aspect of religious common life with the bishop was the beginning of the Canons Regular.

One of the chief difficulties of the African Church at this time was the alarming dearth of clergy. The inroads of the Donatists were so pronounced that many bishops had no subjects fit for priestly ordination. To these bishops it seemed a special act of a loving Providence that Augustine had instituted his monastery where members of the laity were trained in the religious life. It soon became a common thing for the bishops of the province to ask for monks from the monastery at Tagaste in order to ordain them as priests to work in the various dioceses. And Augustine readily acceded to such requests, though this involved a complete change in his point of view when first he sought as a layman to band together other laymen to seek God in solitude.

The new form of religious life attracted people of all kinds, but not all were fit for the advanced perfection of the religious calling. Augustine admitted this:

There are false monks; we, too, know this; but those who profess to be what they are not cannot destroy the blessed brotherhood.

And in his famous *78th Letter,* he writes:

> Although discipline rules in my house, I am a man, and
> live among men. I cannot dare to assert that my house is
> better than the ark of Noah, where one of eight men was
> found reprobate; nor that of Abraham where it was said,
> Expel the handmaiden and her son . . . nor that of Jacob
> . . . nor that of David . . . nor the dwelling place of Paul
> . . . nor that of our Lord Christ wherein eleven good men
> tolerated Judas a thief; nor last, is my house better than
> heaven itself whence fell the angels.

He added:

> I confess simply and sincerely that as I have rarely found
> men better than the good monks, so too, I have never
> found men worse than the bad monks; so that for this rea-
> son I think the Apocolypse says: 'He that is filthy, let him
> be filthy still: and he that is just, let him be justified still"
> (Apoc. xxii. 2).

In another place (Psalms xcix. 11) he compares the monastery to
a safe harbor into which sometimes the winds of the tempest find
an entrance, causing the vessels therein to knock against one another, perhaps even to damage one another; "but must one maintain therefore that they would be better off on the high sea in
the midst of the storm?"

Saint Augustine, the founder, had the joy of seeing his work
carried by his disciples all over North Africa. We know of no
less than nineteen monasteries founded during his lifetime by the
monks who had been nurtured in the Tagastan school. Ten of
these became priests and bishops, of whom Alypius, Profuturus,
Evodius, Possidius and Urbanus, among others, are known to us
by name. He also founded religious houses for women and placed
his own sister at the head of one, which sheltered also two of his
nieces.

\*     \*     \*     \*     \*

The principles of Augustine's monasticism are summed up in
the Rule *"Ad Servos Dei."* There is a lively question whether
this Rule was written first for the nuns or for the monks. We find

it in two forms, one in the *211th Letter* addressed to a convent of nuns, and the other a slightly modified form standing alone in the *Codices,* and called simply "The Rule." Those who maintain that it was written for the nuns point to the *Letter;* those who claim it was written for men bring out the fact that in its simple condition of Rule, apart from any letter, it is found in the oldest manuscripts that we have—certainly older than any of those containing the famous *Letter.* Be it written for men or women, primarily, the Rule of Saint Augustine has had a place of supreme importance in all later religious life in the Church. Saint Benedict, commonly known as the Father of Monasticism in the West, made use of it before he compiled his own excellent Rule. And between them, these two Rules account for almost all the activity in the religious life in Europe until the late Middle Ages. A thesis written at Owens College states:

> The Rule of Saint Augustine is writ large in the records of the Middle Ages. According to the Mediæval tradition it would almost seem that the Fifth Century Saint and Bishop had foreseen and provided for vast fields of activity utterly unknown to his own time. From the Eleventh Century onwards, Augustine's Rule became the standard of nearly every religious community which had a mission beyond the praise of God and the discipline of self. The Canon Regular and the Preaching Friar preached and taught, the Knights of the military Orders fought for religion abroad, the hospital Brother and Sister labored for the relief of sick, poor and leprous at home, while all professedly conforming in life and spirit to the "precepts of their Holy Father, Augustine." From the days of the Hildebrandine Revival to the period of the Renaissance and the Reformation, almost all ordered religious life which was not Benedictine, was Augustinian in character, and the tradition was further emphasized in a post-mediæval movement, the active monasticism of the Counter-Reformation. The Austin Rule came almost to mark off the active from the contemplative Orders.

And Le Mire writes:

> Saint Augustine is called, *par excellence, Magnus Pater* because of the great number of orders and religious con-

gregations spread throughout the world, which are enrolled under his standard and Rule.

It would take more time and space than are at at hand to recall all these Orders. We can but trace the outline and mention some of the outstanding names. We are proud to place first of all our own glorious tradition which traces the Hermit Brethren of Saint Augustine back to that first foundation at Tagaste. When the Vandal ruin already threatening at the time of Saint Augustine's death finally overwhelmed the African Church, these first-born of Augustine crossed the sea to Italy and found the holy place of Lecceto near Siena. There were still the hermits, successors of those visited by Augustine himself long before, at the time of his conversion, when on his journey from Milan returning to Africa. Landucci claims these as the first Hermits of Saint Augustine, and Crusenius makes of the merger of the African fugitives and the residents of "The Hermitage of the Wood" the beginning of our Holy Order in Europe.

Another of Augustine's African followers, Saint Gelasius, came to Rome and there carried the discipline of the Canons Regular and established the Canons of the Lateran. Some of the Chroniclers state that many of the famous abbeys of the early ages, as Lerins, followed the Augustinian Rule, but such is the lack of records for those times that the question must be left open.

Coming to the Twelfth Century, we have the Premonstratensians founded by Saint Norbert in 1120, in the Diocese of Lyons and confirmed by Calixtus II in 1211 under the Rule of Saint Augustine. The great Saint Dominic on founding his mighty Order of Preachers, gave them this same Rule. The Clerks of the Common Life, best remembered today because Thomas à Kempis was a member, used our Rule. The Gesuati and the Scoppettini did likewise, as did the Trinitarians founded by Saint John of Matha, until Innocent III, in the year 1197, gave them a Rule of their own. Pope Gregory IX gave our Rule to the Order of Our Lady of Mercy, founded by Saint Raymond of Pennafort in 1228, and five years later the Servites received it.

Many famous military Orders fought under this Rule. The Knights of Malta, the Teutonic Knights and the Knights of Saint Lazarus are among these. The Knights Hospitaliers of Saint John also follow this Rule of Saint Augustine.

Altogether, Crusenius, writing in 1621, names forty-three Orders and twenty-eight Congregations which then followed the Rule. Of course, many of these have long since disappeared from the pages of history, but others have come to take their places, such as the Ursulines of our day, and many others, who are carrying on the glorious traditions inherited from the great exponent of Monasticism in the West.

# THE CHURCH AND EVOLUTION

SAINT AUGUSTINE, in his instructive work "On Christian Doctrine" tells us that "it is the duty of the interpreter and teacher of Holy Scripture, the defender of the true faith and the opponent of error, both to teach what is right and to refute what is wrong, and in the performance of this task to conciliate the hostile, to arouse the careless, and to tell the ignorant both what is occurring at present and what is probable in the future." (Book IV, Chapter IV, 56.)

That the Church is the interpreter and teacher in matters connected with the inspired text cannot be gainsaid; hence we seem justified in expecting that the Church will teach us all that is required for the proper understanding of the truths revealed to us in this way by the Holy Ghost. But in this we must proceed with caution and patience. For this reason I am inclined to think that the title of this paper will be somewhat misleading, for it seems to promise more than can be offered.

No one has been authorized by the Church to speak in her name. It is true that occasionally some of the members of the Church have spoken and written as though they voiced her teachings; but it is well to remember that the Representative of Christ on earth is capable of fulfilling the mission entrusted to her without dictation from those who pose as her defenders and guides. In the matter of which we are to treat I fear that some well-meaning but, perhaps, misinformed "exponents" of the Catholic doctrine have at times exceeded their office of orthodox exponents of the teaching of the Church. There can be no doubt that they have been impelled by the highest of motives, but they have failed to use the discretion that should characterize those who seek after and defend the truth as it is objectively propounded. It is foreign to my purpose to offer destructive criticism, nor do I assert that their reasoned convictions are wrong; but there is a very great difference between what is true and what is proposed as the formal teaching of the Church as the doctrine to be held as divinely revealed. Hence in this discussion I shall consider the stand of the Church on the question of evolution more from the negative point of view than according to what is positively proposed; with the exception, of course, of those points of doctrine on which the Church has spoken clearly and authoritatively, as will appear in the development of this highly controversial question.

The purpose of this paper is to place before you in brief outline the principles that must be adopted in the solution of the problem. It is a matter of record that the conversion of many has been thwarted or, at least, retarded, and the defection of many from the Faith has been brought about because of the false assertion that certain truths—which to these individuals seem scientifically established—were said to be contrary to the revealed word of God. We have nothing to fear from the findings of the sciences; as a matter of fact, this is one of the ordinary means by which God enables us to understand the fullness of the truth which emanates from Him. Science that is worthy of the name cannot contradict anything that comes to us from a higher source. Although the term "evolution" as well as "transform-ism," etc., may be understood in more than one way, the fact is that the word has taken on a meaning pretty well determined and understood by those who employ it. I think Father O'Brien, in his work entitled *Evolution and Religion,* gives us a better insight into the real meaning of evolution as it is commonly understood by the majority of its proponents. He says "the fundamental meaning of evolution is that there has been a development from simple rudimentary organic life to higher and more complex forms. Functions which were originally performed by a single protoplasmic cell are now discharged by separate organs, highly specialized for that specific task. Evolution represents a progressive march upwards from simple, rudimentary, homogeneous organisms to higher, complex, heterogeneous ones with specialized organs for different functions." I do not ask you to subscribe to this definition, but it seems to represent quite accurately the concept in the minds of the most ardent defenders of this theory.

In order to obviate misunderstandings that may arise from

the use of terms, it seems necessary to advert to the fact that many defenders of evolution are called Darwinists. Strictly speaking, the terms "Evolution" and "Darwinism" are not convertible. The latter may be identified with the former only in a small and contributory way. But since it is not our purpose to find fault with the words used, but rather to consider the thought intended by words that may not, at times, be apt, we shall not insist upon the distinction that really should obtain in this matter. Strictly speaking, the term Darwinism, as employed by the scientist, is intended to indicate the causal agency advanced by Darwin to explain evolution. Darwin considered evolution an established fact, and the causal agency, natural selection, leading to the survival of the fittest. His doctrine appears in his work *The Origin of Species*.

Those who had already bidden farewell to the traditional teaching regarding the Supernatural hailed Darwinism as the liberator of reason; they viewed the new gospel of evolution as essentially heterodox and irreconcilable, not only with the text of Genesis, but also with the doctrine taught by the Apostles. Christianity was deemed incompatible with the findings of science and they did not hesitate to assert that evolution was unquestionably heretical.

Certainly it is not our purpose to encourage such extreme charges against one who has contributed a great deal to our fund of knowledge. Nor, on the other hand do we hold any brief for the writings of this scientist. What is proven to be factual we must accept. What is deduced from the findings of the scientists will be accepted or rejected in accordance with its merits. It is well to remember that in this, as in all other fields, it often happens that a "man's enemies are those of his own household." It is not fair to deny to Darwin the appreciation that his work merited, especially in the field of paleontology and zoology; the rich collection of scientific data he accumulated assuredly gives evidence of his painstaking industry and powers of observation. He is the first naturalist of modern times to set forth in such abundance the marvelous changes wrought in plants and animals by the variations of nutriment, environment, artificial and natural selection, and many other contributing agencies. Had he been content to say that, during the period of formation of the world as we now know it, and in the HYPOTHESIS of the slow and progressive formation of the species, God had availed Himself of natural means, such as heredity, selection, environment, etc., and had made these concur in the action of God in effectuating His plan, I think he would not have have experienced the opposition of so many scholars. For it should not occasion us any surprise that God avails Himself of secondary causes. If the causes enumerated are sufficient to induce remarkable changes in the individuals of a species, we must admit that even greater changes could be effected in the descending groups under the directing hand of God. Thus adapting to his theory that of "evolution under God," Darwin could have avoided the deplorable exaggerations that have vitiated the partial truths of his system. He could not then be accused of marshaling against God the forces of materialism and atheism.

Among Catholics who have interested themselves in this question, we see the name of Rev. J. A. Zahm, formerly a professor of science at Notre Dame University. His works, published in the declining years of the past century, *Bible, Science and Faith* and *Evolution and Dogma,* created a deep impression on students of this question. Viewing the findings of the scientist in this connection as an indication of the providence, power and wisdom of the Creator, he blazed a new trail, greatly at variance with the attitude adopted by Catholic scholars of the contemporary and preceding eras. In 1909 Canon Doderlot, who had written at great length in defense of the new theory, was delegated by the Authorities of Louvain University to represent that Institution at the ceremonies held at Cambridge in honor of Charles Darwin. The words spoken by the Canon on that occasion give us an insight into his appraisal of the author of the *Origin of Species.* He says: "It is no exaggeration to say that, in showing us a creation more grandiose than we had ever expected it, Charles Darwin completed the work of Isaac Newton; because for all those whose ears are not incapable of hearing, Darwin was the interpreter of the organic world, just as Newton was the voice from Heaven come to tell us of the glory of the Creator, and to proclaim that the universe is a work truly worthy of His name."

As the years roll on, the followers of those leaders who sustain some form of evolution are increasing in number. In our Catholic periodicals we frequently observe that those who write on this topic incline to the belief or conviction that evolution in some form is either an established fact, or on the right road to the discovery of the explanation of natural phenomena with respect to the origin and development of life. But no matter what the future has in store for us, we can rest assured that the position of the Catholic Church will never be endangered, nor shall she be compromised. Between faith and science there can be no conflict. The Vatican Council, speaking on this point states: "Although faith is above reason, still there can be no real disagreement between them: since it is the same God who reveals mysteries and infuses faith, who has implanted in the soul the light of reason: God cannot deny Himself, nor can truth contradict truth. Vain appearances of such contradiction arise principally on the score that either the dogmas of faith have not been understood and expounded according to the mind of the Church, or fancies are substituted for the dictates of reason." The Council even goes further and notes the respective functions of faith and reason in the acquisition of profitable knowledge, stating that "right reason demonstrates the foundations of faith and, enlightened by this infused gift, cultivates the science of things Divine, whereas faith frees reason from error and safeguards it and supplies it with much knowledge." Never does the Church dissuade men from embracing scientific truth that is in reality truth. On the contrary, she aids and promotes the sciences. She does not ignore or despise the advantages accruing to man from the cultivation of the sciences, but, rather, she confesses that since these proceed from the God of all knowledge, they should, if rightly used, under the grace of God lead men to their Author. Admitting that reason is entitled to becoming liberty in matters that pertain to its respective field, she warns it against embracing errors that are opposed to divine truth, or, passing beyond due bounds, attacking those things that are of faith.

The claim is frequently made by men versed in the sciences that this field is exclusively theirs, and that philosophers or theologians should not intrude therein. If they would stop to reason a moment they would realize that all the sciences, whether physical, philosophical or theological have their origin, *as sciences,* in human reason. And since this prerogative is reserved to no particular class of human beings, whether they be naturalists, philosophers or theologians, we must admit that all have the right to pass judgment upon the relation between premises and conclusions, provided they have qualified by careful study to act in the capacity of judge. We grant that it is the province of the scientists to discover and, to the best of their ability, explain the facts; but we reserve to ourselves as philosophers or theologians the right to pass judgment upon the validity of the reasoning upon the facts that are submitted.

A rather striking paradox occurs to us in this connection. At the present time many Darwinists appeal to the law known as the *Mendelian Law of Heredity* as an explanation of the causes of the mechanics of evolution. Gregor Mendel (1822-1884) was not only a scholar of note, but also a priest, well acquainted with theology, a member of the Augustinian Monastery in Brünn, later Superior. For fifteen years he taught natural history in the School at Brünn and carried out thousands of experiments in the cloister-garden. At the age of forty-three he published his work at Brünn but his findings attracted little attention until they were rediscovered and published for the benefit of the modern scientific world by Professor Hugo de Vries of Holland, in 1900. It is admitted by scholars that the facts discovered by Mendel and interpreted in the way shown by him, have revolutionized biological ideas in certain directions. Since the laws in nature which govern the processes of heredity were long and eagerly sought after by scientists, we can easily understand the enthusiastic greeting accorded the discovery by the scientists of our own century, and we can grasp the import of this law to the doctrine of evolution, which is mainly concerned with the development of life in the individual and species. According to the old doctrine, the law of heredity was considered by scholars, in the main, to be one of specific constancy. According to modern schools, however, whose forerunners and principal exponents were Lamarck and Darwin, the law of heredity is one of progressive and indefinite variation.

The discussions on Evolution and Transformism have overturned so many former philosophical notions and have bred such disorder and confusion in the minds of so many thinkers, that it is absurd for us to look for a complete and perfect solution of all the questions involved in the near or even remote future. It is a source of consolation, however, that able men approach the question with calmer minds and less prejudice than marked the leaders of thought a few generations ago. The time has arrived for the philosopher and theologian to call to mind the principles upon which all true knowledge is based, and which the scientists should never forget; to determine the point of doctrine involved; to recapitulate and extract, as well as to coördinate the conclusions worth while with respect to natural science, philosophy and theology; to evaluate dispassionately the philosophical and theological import of the solutions proposed.

All scientists and the majority of philosophers and theologians are convinced that this terrestrial globe, which we call our present home, carries in itself, either directly or by implication, the story of its origin and development. Unfortunately the gigantic pages of this story-book are unwieldly and thus are unfolded with the greatest difficulty; the leaves of the book are hidden deep in the bowels of the earth and are comparatively rare, and discovered only at the cost of great effort. Even when certain fundamental facts concerning this mysterious book are unearthed, their character and style, although not altogether undecipherable by man, contain enigmas and obscurities whose significance has not yet been thoroughly grasped.

I need not explain in detail the suggestion proposed by Kant, Laplace and others, known as the Nebular Hypothesis, which has gained acceptance. According to this explanation we know that the earth was not always inhabited, since the material world was forced to undergo transformations that were altogether incompatible with any form of organic life. In due time, the length of which we cannot even attempt to guess, the primal forms of vegetable and animal life appeared. The first studies made by naturalists seemed to indicate, from the examination of the flora and fauna, not only differences among the ascending strata, but even mutual independence. This led many scientists, such as Cuvier, Milne Edwards, etc., to assume that the Divine Architect had effected multiple and successive creations, thereby explaining the apparent continuity of life and the gradual ascent in the line of perfection.

Naturally this explanation failed to satisfy those restive spirits who, led by materialistic and atheistic antagonism to a Deity, refused to admit the interference or intervention of God; nor was it more acceptable to others who, though convinced of its possibility, hoped to find in this series of beings a geometrical gradation and almost imperceptible transition from less perfect to more perfect organisms, effectuating an ideal plan conceived in the mind of the Creator.

Adherents of both these schools, then, set out in quest of intermediate types that would convincingly prove the unity and continuity of their broken chain. The first group has long since raised the cry of victory, and this is attested in the very school books wherein evolution is no longer treated as a theory but as an established fact. The second group, realizing that the hypothesis has not been transformed into a thesis, believe that the time is not far-distant, when they will be able to glory in the success which must crown their efforts. In this class, we have, as we shall see in the development of this question, many Catholic scholars. But it is evident that they intend to arrive at the same conclusion from premises that are entirely orthodox.

Now, if science succeeds in proving the actual existence, in

past ages, of these intermediate types, what would be the import
of this discovery? What philosophical and theological consequences would flow from these findings? The ideas of many of
our contemporaries seem greatly confused, and are certainly con-
fusing to the rank and file of the laity and even of the clergy.
Because of the importance of this phase of the question, I think
it advisable to consider the matter in its principal phases, as
far as a short discussion will permit. Since this is a highly controversial question, I deem it only fair that those who differ
with us on many points should receive a proper hearing.

## I. Stability of Species

Since all evolutionary hypotheses deal with species, it would
be well if we could understand what is meant by species in this
connection. What is the sense and value of the principle of "Stability or constancy of species"? According to many contemporaries this rule, just as many others of the physical and
metaphysical orders, is to be relegated to the heap of discarded
theories by which the ancients were influenced. It is not necessary for us to treat in detail of the many meanings this word
has taken on in the course of history. Species as understood
by the older exegetes and the schoolmen before discussion of this
nature arose will not concern us at the present time. We restrict
the limits to species of the biological order. As far as the biological concept of species is concerned, we are forced to admit
that in the light of present-day knowledge it is extremely difficult
to determine just how far the limits of any given species extend.
But until something demonstrative of the contrary is advanced,
we feel justified in aligning ourselves with those who favor
fixity of species in the sense outlined in the following pages.
Our understanding of the matter under consideration is based
upon a very simple axiom, and upon quite obvious facts of
observation. The axiom is this: A being employing the powers
naturally inherent in it, cannot develop a faculty that it has
received in potency. The facts of observation are these: In
the world in which we live, created beings have not received

unlimited powers. Each one possesses a certain degree of entity, power or perfection and the highest degree determines the place that being is to occupy in the scale of living things, and this determination we call a species. Species, therefore, is fixed in the sense that a thing cannot, by means of its own powers, extend itself beyond the sphere of activity to which it has been assigned. For example, a mustard seed can produce only a tree of that nature and never a fish, a bird or a horse.

In the present state of our knowledge, is it possible to render a definition that would serve as an absolute and adequate criterion by which to judge in every case whether two things belong to the same species, and by which the species may be distinguished from the race? I should not like to dogmatize in this obscure matter, for such a criterion would involve a more intimate and complete knowledge of these individual objects than we seem to have at the present time. Darwin, who had written a volume on the origin of species gave it as his view that the idea of species was "undefinable." His dictum is approved by many. In passing I may observe that thorough-going evolutionists may consistently ignore any determination of classes, orders, genera, etc., but this easy way can hardly be adopted with any degree of logic by those who refuse to subscribe to evolution as it is propounded by Darwin and his followers.

Following the lines laid down by men preëminent in the fields of Natural Science and of Philosophy, I think we can render a definition sufficiently exact from a speculative point of view, although in practice, as stated before, it may not be so easy to point out the line of demarcation. Professor Poulton defines species as "an interbreeding community." Father Albert Farges defines species as "a collection or group of individuals bearing a resemblance to one another, grounded upon a basic, inalienable, common type according to which they are fashioned." Developing this definition, it may be stated that a species is:

1. A group of living individuals fundamentally like unto one another, and differing from other groups of living things.

2. These individuals are incapable of variation or natural perfection beyond certain limits which are insurmountable.

3. These individuals are capable of conserving and perpetuating their basic type, of defending it against assaults, and of reëstablishing it when violent encroachments against nature have disfigured it.

Perhaps this last mentioned criterion is of little avail in paleontological species. Many experts claim that such a criterion is worthless in the plant world, in which many exceptions are said to occur. Men versed in this science assure us that within the species itself the fertility always maintains the same general level, while by the crossing of different "species" it diminishes very considerably. This does not, of necessity, militate against what has been stated regarding species. Deterioration of offspring and subsequent sterility in the latter may be explained by the weakness of the stock. However, the crossing of which the botanists speak may have been effected between species that are called systematic, rather than between fundamental or natural species. If such be the case, these instances do not form an argument against the properties of species in the radical sense of the term. Perhaps the explanation may become clearer if, instead of using the terms "systematic species" and "Natural or fundamental species" the changes in each class be referred to as "minor evolution" and "major evolution," to employ terms proposed by Arnold Lunn. "The changes within a species (e. g., the variation of the horse from Eohippus to Equus) might be described as minor evolution, and the transformation of one species into another (e. g., reptile into bird) as major evolution." Dewar suggests that we use the term "evolution" for the latter and "differentiation" for the former. If such exactness were employed many of the misunderstandings would be cleared up. We must remember, however, that the variability of members of a species which is restricted to encroachments contrary to nature, or to artificial processes and the intervention of man, will hardly prove anything. At least, it will not explain the production of species that appeared before man was made, nor that which is natural. And this is the problem confronting the scientists. Therefore, to know whether the constancy of species is a law of nature, it is necessary to observe and interpret facts that occur, or have occurred, independently of human intervention or other things that may perturb the course of nature, in so far as this observation is possible. It is necessary to observe what takes place at the present time, and endeavor to determine what occurred in prehistoric periods, in all the epochs of the earth's development, in all climes and environments. Certainly at the present time, and by this I mean to include all valid historical accounts of which we have any record, one species (fundamental or natural species) does not transform itself into another higher species. Now to conclude that thousands or millions of centuries, or millions of generations are required to effect such a change, seems to be a deduction that is mostly gratuitous. The mummies of Egypt, dating back several thousands of years prove the existence of individuals like, in every essential respect, to those that inhabit the earth today. If thousands of years have not effected any change in these types, we seem to assume too much when we admit that a multiplication of like periods would bring about a different result. This reasoning seems to be substantiated by the discoveries of the paleontologists. Many species that existed in the quarternary and tertiary epochs, yes, even in the secondary and primary, are like to those of the present day, without even the slightest change.

Hence it seems that the law of stability, if we are to derive any positive information from the interpretation of facts, is the law that governs the actual world of material living beings. At least, in the present status of the question, it is based upon objective proof more cogent than the theory of basic transformation. It is well for us to bear in mind that genetic connection among the species as known to us today is assumed by many evolutionists, and admitted by such, to be merely a "postulate of the evolutionary doctrine," subject to rejection upon the discovery of some other explanation that will fit the general plan of evolution.

Professor Delage, who applauded Darwin because he "explained the seemingly marvellous adaptations of living things by the mere action of natural factors without looking to a Divine intervention, without resorting to any finalist or metaphysical hypothesis," declared that "if there were some other scientific hypothesis besides that of *descent* to explain the origin of species, many transformists would abandon their present opinion as not being sufficiently demonstrated . . . If one takes one's stand upon *the exclusive ground of facts,* it must be acknowledged that the formation of one species from another species has not been demonstrated at all." From these words of Delage it would seem that the principal objection to the old theory is the intervention of the Creator or the presence of finality in the kingdoms of living things. Fundamentally, the objection against stability is, that it would involve a continuous multiplication of miracles. These objections, coming from materialists who explain effects without adequate causes, who postulate motion without a prime Mover, who prate about the contingent but deny the Absolute, and who ascribe to the material universe attributes that they deny to an Intelligent Author, can easily be understood when we realize the nature of the bias by which they are influenced. Such objections, however, cannot be consistently made by scholars who understand the truth of the real origin of things. If God were to intervene in the formation of the world after its creation, and in particular in the determination of the graded species, such act on the part of God would in no-wise constitute a miracle, as explained elsewhere in this article. Admittedly God would act as Administrator, as pointed out by Saint Augustine, completing in time the work He decreed from the beginning; but such assistance could not be described as creation in the proper sense, nor as a supernatural act, as theologians understand this term. It would not be contrary to nature, since its purpose would be to establish in nature a definite order, to accord to the world the natural perfection which is congruous, and to lead it to the heights intended by God in the creative act. That which is really difficult to understand, on which account it is rejected by rationalistic scientists, is the fundamental factor in all these developments: that is, Divine intervention itself, as synonymous with creation. There can be no doubt at all that herein is contained a most profound mystery, which we accept, not as a postulate, but as something known to us with such certainty as to exclude all doubt or misgivings. If a miracle involves an exception to, or suspension of the law of nature, I think we are justified in asserting that in the "major evolution" we have a most remarkable miracle consisting in the exception to the law of change, since so many species have remained stable throughout the course of the geological ages and the periods of history of which we have sufficiently complete accounts. I wish it understood, however, that the stability of which I have been speaking cannot be put forth as the opinion of all theologians. It seems that the old-fashioned opinion of fixity is experiencing strong opposition from present-day writers among Catholic authors.

On the other hand, though, Fixism is defended by some who are not at all affected by Catholic influence, and certainly are not Catholic in sentiment. Professor Bateson declares: "Analysis has revealed hosts of transferable characters. Their combinations suffice to supply in abundance series of types which might pass for new species and certainly would be so classed if they were met with in nature. Yet, critically tested, we find that they are not distinct species, and we have no reason to suppose that any accumulation of characters of the same order would culminate in the production of distinct species." Reaction against monophyletic evolution is seen in an outstanding contribution, NONO-GENESIS, by Dr. Berg. The latter has set forth evidence of the falsity of many contentions supported at the present time. He is a Russian scientist in the employ of the Soviet Government. As is known to all, the Republic of the Soviet is decidedly atheistic, and has employed all the artifices of science and all branches of learning to supplant a Creator in the minds of the people. Hence we may look upon Berg as non-suspect, in so far as Religion and Theistic principles are concerned. "A strict adherence to the monophyletic principle," he says, "is generally bound to lead to absurdity . . . to support the view that animals descended from four or five progenitors is now impossible; the number of the primal ancestors must be computed in thousands or tens of thousands." Again he states: "It is truly remarkable that Paleontology in no way displays transitional forms between phyla and classes, and, possibly, not even between orders. Thus we are ignorant of transitional forms, not only between vertebrates and invertebrates, fishes and tetrapods, but even between the cartilaginous (such as sharks) and higher fishes; in spite of a wonderful affinity between reptiles and birds, no transitional forms are known hitherto. Formerly, this circumstance was accounted for by the imperfection of the geological record; but it is none the less surprising that the deeper our knowledge penetrates into the domain of fossils, the farther back recede genetic inter-relations, which, as it were, ever elude our grasp."

\*　　\*　　\*　　\*　　\*

Now we must ask whether the FACT of evolution has been established, and, if so, to what extent; that is, whether it has been proved to be a certainty, or, at least, sufficiently probable.

As a preamble to this part of the discussion it is deemed expedient to accept the distinctions and divisions found in the books of science dealing with life in its lower forms. No one, except a sceptic, will deny that the inanimate is distinct from the animate. These latter, furthermore, are rightly divided into plants and animals, and are treated in the schools under separate heads so as to constitute distinct branches of natural sciences. Both kingdoms are again divided by systems, agreeing in their main features, into stocks, classes, orders, families, genera, species, sub-species and so on.

Since we are not called upon to prove what has been discovered and explained for our benefit by the natural scientists, I take the liberty of treating these kingdoms in the inverse order, so as to arrive at the "beginnings," which are of paramount importance, and involve principles that in some way are related to Philosophy, Exegesis, and Theology.

1.　Textbooks on Zoology divide the animal kingdom into

several families, ranging in number from seven to ten, according to the view of the individual author, and they give evidence of some kind of distinction between members of this kingdom, and those of the lower group, plants. The numerical divisions do not concern us to any great extent at this particular time, but we are deeply interested in the nature of the distinction (as well as difference) which prevails between the two kingdoms. When we speak of animals we always have in mind organisms endowed with the power of feeling and consciousness. Many evolutionists disregard the difference between the mere living organism and the one endowed with feeling; or, if they admit the difference, they consider it as of secondary importance. But we are not justified in viewing it in this light. We are constrained to admit, in the face of overwhelming evidence, that the psyche or form of the animal is entirely different from that of the plant, and that by means of this higher form of vital activity the animal is able to experience sensation and display more or less "voluntary" power of action. Now if a plant were to be transformed into an animal, the whole nature of its principle would have to be changed. It seems that this would of necessity entail the destruction of the vital principle of the plant and the insertion of the psyche of the animal, excluding, thereby, all genetic connection between the extremes. For this reason many evolutionists, admitting the essential difference between the two kingdoms, postulate in the respective classes certain fundamental types from which all the families gradually emerge.

2. Now a few words about the lowest form of life—vegetable life. Biologists tell us that life is a particular kind of activity that distinguishes organisms from things in general and from machines. They admit that there is obviously a great difference between thoroughly living creatures (organisms) and undeniably not-living things, as stones and crystals. "But," states J. Arthur Thompson, "it is not at present possible to say what the most important or fundamental difference is." Living, according to these authorities, is a kind of activity consisting of action and reaction between the organism and its environment, and

directed towards securing either self-maintenance or the continuance of the race. Essential to living creatures, from the chemicophysical point of view is correlation. The chemical processes work into one another's hands, so that in spite of ceaseless change the organism persists in its integrity for days or years or cycles of years. In other words, what goes on is correlated or coördinated so as to secure self-preservation for a longer or shorter time— for a few days in a midge, for two thousand years in some of the great Sequoia trees. There is no analogue to this in the inorganic domain (Thompson). Admitting then, a fundamental, or, according to our view, an essential difference between inorganic and organic substance, are we justified in asserting that the latter proceeded from the former? That life arises spontaneously from non-living matter has been frequently declared by those who are inclined to go to extremes in upholding evolution. It is looked upon as a postulate of science; a philosophical need, as O. Hertwig states. Haeckel, in commenting upon this assures us that "We must regard this hypothesis as the immediate consequence and the necessary completion of the generally accepted theory of Kant and Laplace; and we find therein, in the totality of natural phenomena, such a compelling logical necessity that we must therefore regard this deduction, which to many seems a bold one, as incontrovertible."

Thompson thus expresses his view on the origin of life: After the earth became cool enough to be a home of organisms they appeared. How are we to think of their origin? (a) From ancient times it has been a favorite answer that the dust of the earth became vital in a manner which cannot be described in terms of natural science. But this is to foreclose the problem prematurely. (b) It has been suggested that minute organisms came to the earth from elsewhere, deep in the cracks of a meteorite or among cosmic dust. This is possible, though not perhaps likely; and in any case it only shifts the problem from the earth to some other scene. (c) the possibility remains that living organisms may have evolved from non-living material, e. g., from some colloidal carbonaceous slime in which ferments were operative.

"There seems to be in nature, inorganic as well as organic, a tendency to complexity. Corpuscles are believed to have combined to form atoms, and atoms molecules, and small molecules large ones, and large molecules colloid masses. Perhaps this complexity resulted in the evolution of organisms. But there is no indication of such a process going on today, and we do not know of any living substance apart from organisms or pieces of them. It is usual to point to the achievements of the synthetic chemist who is able from simple substances to build up complex substances like oxalic acid, indigo, caffeine, and grape sugar. As yet there has been no synthesis of proteids—those complex compounds which form a universal and essential part of the physical basis of life." Then citing several suggestions as to the way in which the physical basis of life might be formed, especially those proposed by Verworn, Snyder and Prof. Benjamin Moore, he concludes: "None of these theories on the origin of life is in a form ready for acceptance. If, however, there is mentality and reason at the end of the long process, it must have been in some manner present in kind in the beginning also—a purely matter-and-motion evolution theory is impossible."

J. B. S. Haldane, who, in 1922, became a Reader in Bio-Chemistry at Cambridge and ten years later a Fellow of the Royal Society, writing in 1935 says: "I see nothing improbable in spontaneous generation. It was generally believed in until the eighteenth century by theists and atheists alike. Pasteur and others showed that the alleged generation of organisms large enough to be seen with a microscope did not occur when proper precautions were taken. But it would be very surprising if such relatively large organisms did start from scratch, so to say. If there is spontaneous generation it is almost certainly of much simpler living things, such as filterpassing viruses. . . . Probably chemists have not yet produced a living cell in the laboratory. They have produced cell-like structures showing some of the phenomena of life, such as orderly pattern, growth and division, but these structures if they are alive at all (which is perhaps a matter of definition), certainly cannot carry on life indefinitely, any more than the sexless flies. . . . However, chemists are gradually producing the phenomena regarded as the characteristics of life. It was said that only vital force could make organic compounds. In 1828 Wöhler made the first in the laboratory, and now hundreds of thousands have been made. Pasteur said that fermentation was impossible without life. Buchner disproved him. We can already make many parts of the living cell, though not the majority. When chemists have either found some which present insuperable difficulties in manufacture, or have made them all but have been unable to put them together as a going concern, it will be time to twit them with their lack of success. Meanwhile biochemistry goes on steadily in spite of your assertion of its failure. There is reason to think that a representative cell contains over ten thousand, but less than a million, distinct chemical substances. When there are ten thousand bio-chemists in the world it will be time to ask them to make a cell."

The latest pronouncements, as far as I know, have come from Professors who are members of the American Association for the Advancement of Sciences. Dr. Oscar Riddle, Carnegie Institution biologist, states: The two questions of the origin of life upon earth and of the origin of consciousness or mind in animal series are complementary to Darwin's principle, first conceived in 1835 and published in 1859 . . . Scientists since then, he says, have discovered how nature, under ordinary temperature and under solar radiations, creates organic substances, like sugars, from water and carbon dioxide gas. Such a sugar, glucose, in alkaline solution and with plenty of time, has been changed into hundreds of organic substances. In his address to the Association he declared that a new clue to life's beginning was found in the preparation made by Dr. W. M. Stanley, of the Rockefeller Institute for Medical Research. This preparation consisted in a crystallized tobacco mosaic virus which is apparently a link between living and non-living things. This virus is a mechanism by which the basic evolutionary process may have occurred—virus substance which has the properties of both animate and inanimate things. By itself Dr. Stanley's tobacco mosaic virus is a protein apparently as non-living as a piece of rock, but when brought into contact with a proper piece of living tissue it is able to grow and propagate itself and it then seemingly exhibits only this single characteristic of living matter. The virus protein is similar to the genes which are the units of heredity carried on the chromosones. Both are beyond the range of the strongest microscope and differ neither greatly nor consistently in size. Thus, Dr. Riddle said, "the bridge between living and non-living things may be shorter than we have imagined. The missing span may be only that which connects sugars and amino acids which are known to form spontaneously and a protein molecule like that of a virus or gene. Life may have begun in some such manner by the simple addition of just one element not previously in inanimate things." Professor Arthur H. Compton, of the University of Chicago, thinks that cosmic rays and other celestial radiations were the actual creators of life. It is his belief that these rays change the nucleus of sex cells of plants, animals and human beings; in this way heredity is changed and new breeds and races arise.

Now this description of the origin of life in its earliest form necessitates the consideration of the much mooted question of what is called, for want of a better name, "spontaneous generation." It is also known under the fanciful names of abiogenesis, heterogenesis, autogenesis, archebiosis, etc. The words are not used by all authors in the same sense. But it is not my purpose to quibble on the use of words or phrases. After all, these are nothing but the ordinary vehicles by which we make known our thoughts, and we know from experience that new meanings and better meanings may be attached to expressions that formerly conveyed another thought. It is unfortunate, of course, that in questions of this nature, unchanging terminology is not employed. But we are faced with this condition, and it is our duty, as lovers of the truth, to endeavor to discern the real meaning of authors whose vocabulary does not coincide with our own. With this in mind, we may now ask, whether spontaneous (or, equivocal, as it is called by many) generation may be admitted as the logical and actual explanation of the origin of life in its lower forms. Father

John O'Brien, Professor in the Newman Foundation at the University of Illinois, and Father Ernest C. Messenger, a noted scholar, who have rendered masterful contributions to the topic of evolution, inform us that all history discloses that the Christian philosophers from the days of Saint Basil in the fourth century, to the discovery of Pasteur in the nineteenth, universally believed in the spontaneous generation of certain forms of life from dead matter. Criticism is made to the effect that these, and other Catholic writers have set at naught the teaching of philosophers of the past and present century. That such was not their intention is clear, I think, from a careful perusal of their opinions on this point. They merely place emphasis on a point that was not developed fully enough by earlier writers. Take, for example, the method in which the question is treated by Reinstadler in his excellent work on Anthropology: "We must admit, and Virchow concedes this point, that spontaneous (equivocal) generation is defended by the materialists not as a truth that has really been proved, but as a "postulate," or invention of their natural philosophy. It is necessary that he who is unwilling to admit that the world was created by God have recourse to spontaneous generation, lest he seem to offer no explanation at all. Since we may not resort to infinite progress in a series of cells produced by their predecessors, the true postulate of science demands that we admit that the first cell was *either* immediately produced by the Creator, *or,* if you prefer, produced from inorganic matter under the influx of the Creator. We do not deny that these first cells could have originated in *some way* (ullo modo) from inorganic matter; indeed we further grant that these cells were not created from nothing, but in fact proceeded from matter already existing, provided it be admitted that these germs did not spring spontaneously from the exclusive powers of inorganic matter (ex solis anorganicæ materiæ viribus). For spontaneous generation of this kind is at variance with the findings of science and with the facts themselves. Since, therefore, organic matter did not always exist, and could not have sprung spontaneously from inorganic matter, it is necessary to admit an extramundane cause by Whom it was produced from *inorganic* (matter). Consequently, the existence of a Supreme Being, the Creator of this world, is *the* "postulate of science."

It is clear that the purpose of this philosopher, as well as of all men who are willing to be guided by the natural light of reason, is to ascribe to the ultimate source all power that is found in creatures. It is universally conceded by Catholic philosophers that God frequently employs natural agents in accomplishing things He could, if He so wished, do immediately by a single act of His will. We know that He uses human agents as His ambassadors, and employs things of a lower nature as instruments for the sanctification of the spiritual soul. Could He not have entrusted to matter the powers that are needed for the proper development of the universe which He created ex nihilo? If the philosophers placed greater insistence on the denial and refutation of that form of materialism and atheism that ascribed to chance, or to any other agency, the power we assert to come from God, we can hardly conclude that they denied the possibility of such a process, provided we admit a sufficient reason for all the activity displayed in nature. Usually the philosophers of the schools are consistent, and when they refute spontaneous generation as the explanation of the origin of life at the beginning or even at the present stage of the world's development, they do so with the understanding that abiogenesis excludes God. That there is justification of their stand can easily be seen if we recall the attitude of many who were opposed to Christian thought as the bulwark reared to prevent progress in scientific knowledge. Hence when the later Scholastics, with this in mind, maintained that spontaneous generation was impossible they did so on the ground that this doctrine was diametrically opposed to the very first principles of science and logic. And in this respect they were right. If, however, we interpret spontaneous generation to mean what recent Catholic proponents of evolution claim for it, I think we have a discussion on words rather than on realities when any real dissension is proclaimed, and the subject matter is too important to engage in such trivialities.

With this in mind we may consider the real crux of the problem and endeavor to determine to our own satisfaction what is the real nature of this generation which is advanced by recent writers as disclosing the views of the greatest thinkers of the golden age of Patrology. Since Saint Augustine is cited in support of the contention that is made in this respect, I deem it my privilege to consider briefly the mind of the Doctor of Grace on the point under treatment. It is not my desire to ignore the other great Doctors who have made clear their thoughts on this subject, such as Saint Ambrose, Saint John Chrysostom, Saint Basil, Saint Gregory of Nyssa, Saint Ephrem, etc., but the limits of this article demand that I refrain from commenting upon all, and obvious reasons constrain me to direct my efforts to the consideration of the views of the one to whom as our Holy Founder we owe special allegiance.

No matter who may be the author of a great and voluminous work, whether he be Divine (as in the case of Sacred Scripture), or human, as in the case of philosophers, theologians and scientists, it is a foregone conclusion that his dicta will be questioned regarding their meaning in very many instances. This is the condition of man. Anyone acquainted with the numerous norms laid down in hermeneutics will realize the truth of this. Regardless of the agreement that prevails among us as to the laws that are to be followed in the matter of interpreting the sense of a text, the fact still remains that capable interpreters often derive opposite meanings from a given document. This is, unfortunately, true with regard to the teaching of the Bishop of Hippo as set forth in his monumental works, *De Genesi ad literam* and *De Trinitate*. I mention only these two works, for they treat quite specifically of the matter in which we are interested at the present time. In order to justify our deductions from the writings of Saint Augustine, we shall quote a few passages from the above named masterpieces which have a direct bearing upon this question.

In the work on "The Trinity" we read:

> In truth, some hidden seeds of all things that are born corporeally and visibly are concealed in the corporeal ele-

ments of this world. For those seeds that are visible now to our eyes from fruits and living things, are quite distinct from the hidden seeds of those former seeds; from which, at the bidding of the Creator, the water produced the first swimming creatures and fowl, and the earth the first buds after their kind, and the first animals after their kind. . . . For, consider, the very least shoot is a seed . . . but of this shoot there is a yet more subtle seed in some grain of the same species, and this is visible even to us. But of this grain there is still further a seed which, although we are unable to see it with our eyes, yet we can conjecture its existence from our reason; because, unless there were some such power in those elements, there would not so frequently be produced from the earth things which had not been sown there; nor yet so many animals, without any previous commixture of male and female; whether on the land, or in the water, which yet grow, and by commingling bring forth others, while they themselves sprang up without any union of parents.—(*De Trin.*, Chap. VIII, 13.)

It is one thing to make and administer the creature from the innermost and highest turning-point of causation, which He alone does who is God the Creator; but quite another thing to apply some operation from without in accordance with the forces and capacities supplied by Him, so that what is created may come forth into being at this time or that, and in this or that way. For all these things have been created already originally and primordially in a kind of weaving together of the elements but they come forth at the opportune time. For as mothers are pregnant with their offspring, so the world itself is pregnant with the causes of things that are born; which are not created in it, except from that highest essence, where nothing either springs up or dies, either begins to be or ceases. But the applying from without of adventitious causes, which, although they are not natural, yet are to be applied according to nature, in order that those things which are contained and hidden in the secret bosom of nature may break forth and be outwardly created in some way by the unfolding of the proper measures and numbers and weights which they have received in secret from Him, "Who has ordered all things in number and measure and weight"; this is not only in the power of bad angels, but also of bad men, as I have shown above.—(*De Trin.*, Chap. IX, 16.)

In his *De Genesi ad literam*, he writes:

In that tiny grain there is a very wonderful and excellent force, by which the neighboring moisture, mixed with earth and thus forming a kind of material, is able to be converted into the character of this tree. . . . So with the animals: it may be uncertain whether they are from seed, or seed from them, but whichever of these was first, it is most certain that it came from earth.

But, as in that grain of seed there were together invisibly all those things that develop into a tree in the course of time, so we must think of the world as having together, when God created all things at once, all those things which were made in it and with it when the day was made—not only the heavens with the sun, moon and stars, with their rotary motion, and the earth and the depths, which undergo variable motions, and the lower parts of the world, but also those things which the waters and the earth produced potentially and causally before they were to arise in the course of time as they are now known to us, in those works which God works until now.—(*De Gen. ad lit.*, Lib. V.)

It is said that the earth produced the grass and trees causally, that is, that it received the power to produce them. In it, as in their roots, so to speak, those things were already made which were to come forth in the course of time: for God planted, indeed, a Paradise to the East . . . and still it is not necessary to say that He added anything to His creation which He had not made before.

All the essences of shrubs and trees were made in the first state, from which (first formation of things) God rested, applying direction and administering, throughout the course of time, those things which He created.

On the fifth day the waters, endowed with their own nature, produced their denizens, that is, all swimming things according to the word of God; and it did this potentially. . . . On the sixth day in like manner the terrestrial animals as from the last element of the world were to be the last, but they (were made) potentially, whose forms time was to unfold later on in a visible manner.—(*De Gen. ad lit.*, Lib. V.)

This entire course of nature, to which we are most accustomed, has certain natural laws proper to itself, according to which even the soul, which is a creature, has certain particular tendencies which in a certain way are so determined that not even a bad will can go beyond them. And the elements of this corporeal world have in themselves their definitive energy and quality, which determines what each can do or not do and what can be done with each, and what cannot be done. And from these beginnings, as it were, all things that are produced, each in its own time, attain their birth and development, to which succeeds decadence and death, according to its kind. Whence it comes about that from a grain of wheat a bean is not generated, nor wheat from the bean: of a brute animal man is not born, nor of man a brute. But beyond this natural course of things, the power of the Creator has reserved to itself the faculty of doing with all these what the seminal reasons themselves cannot do; not however, that which He did not provide for, so that He might be able to make such disposition of them. For His power is not indiscreet, but omnipotent in its wisdom; and thus He does with each thing in its own time what He had provided, beforehand, He could do in it. There is, therefore, another procedure in nature by which a given herb germinates in one manner and another herb in another; by which offspring can be borne in one period of life and not in another; by which man can speak, but the brute cannot. The reasons for these and other like manners of procedure found in things repose not only in God, but are, also, inserted by Him in the things of nature and created with them. In order, therefore, that a tree cut from the ground, dried out and smoothed, without roots, without soil or water suddenly bloom, that one who in her youth was sterile may in her old age beget children, that an ass may speak, and similar occurrences may take place, God, Who created the respective natures, provided that in these natures such things should be possible—nor with these would God have done anything which He determined could not have been done, for He is not more powerful than Himself. However He gave to these things a power in a manner different (from their seminal reasons), that is, He gave it to them in such a manner that it did not reside in their natural activity; but in such a manner were they created that their natures were further subject to a more powerful Will. God therefore retains hidden in Himself the causes of some deeds which (causes) He did not insert in created things and He brings these to fulfillment not by that work of Providence by which He established them in existence, but by that with which He administers, as He wishes, those very things that were created by Him in the manner chosen by Him.—(*De Gen. ad lit.*, Lib. IX.)

Saint Augustine expounds even more extensively his views on seminal reasons in the Sixth Book of the same work. But for the sake of brevity I shall take only the few excerpts quoted above and endeavor to propound the views that seem to accord with the Holy Doctor's on the nature of these seminal reasons, as well as other pertinent matters intimately connected with evolution as it is accepted by so many Catholic scholars at the present time.

At the outset it is well to bear in mind that the questions which agitate the minds of scholars of the present day were not treated by Augustine in the fifth century. The great Bishop was deprived of the knowledge at our disposal regarding Geology, Paleontology, Physics, Chemistry and many other sciences which have added to our fund of profitable knowledge; had he been able to avail himself of the findings of the sciences as we have them now, there can be no doubt that he would have rendered great assistance in the interpretation and explanation of the mysterious phenomena of the universe. Hence, it is hardly fair to ask whether Augustine was an evolutionist as we understand the theory now. However, since the solution of the problem can be brought about only by the proper application of principles, and since these may be formulated by a genius as the result of observation, even of a comparatively few facts, and of the proper use of a highly developed mind, we may expect to find in Augustine's writings certain directive norms which will aid us in handling this difficult problem, in the development of which we are faced, at times, with the same situation that confronted Augustine and occasioned the publication of the great work *De Genesi ad Literam.* He tells us in the work itself (Book I, Chap. 21; Book IX, Chap. 12) that it is his purpose to render an exact and convincing explanation of the sacred text of Genesis in order to defend it against the delirious utterances of the Manicheans. He treats the question according to the three grades of light that were at hand: light borrowed from the sciences, which certainly were meager in their contributions; the light of reason; and the light of Faith. He sets forth clearly that all things come from God by creation, and the immediate effect of this was the *materia informis*. Many present day authorities represent this primordial matter as having first existed in a highly rarified nebular condition. Augustine seems to go even further and designates it as "almost nothing": *prope nihil;* and it would be from these beginnings that all the beings that inhabit this terrestrial planet of ours (that is, all the plants and animals, for we are concerned only with them now), starting from a primitive, seminal, latent state, would have begun the slow process of their development until they arrived at the degree of perfection intended for them by the Creator.

Now in order to understand the relation of Augustine's doctrine to evolution, I think it necessary to propose certain pertinent questions, the proper solution of which will determine the compatibility or incompatibility of the old and the new teaching:

1. What is the nature of the *rationes seminales?*
2. Is spontaneous generation consistent with Augustine's views?
3. May we, under the leadership of Augustine, admit the transformation of species?

1. Although the Holy Doctor frequently uses the term *"rationes seminales"* and terms intended by him to be the equivalent of the same, it is difficult to understand, and harder to explain, the full import of these agencies, whether considered in themselves or in accordance with the part they play in the development of the primordial mass. There can be no reasonable doubt regarding their lack of identity with seeds of vegetables as we know them now, or with the eggs that are now formed in animals that produce their young by this means; for in the event of the contrary being true Augustine would not have said that the earth

had received the power of producing (*virtutem producendi*). Nor may we admit that this power connotes a force that is purely mechanical, for it is obvious to all that life, even in its lowest form, implies something beyond mere mechanical motion. Hence many are of the opinion that these potential germs and seminal reasons designate certain forms, determinants or active powers and were committed to the water and the earth in the beginning, which, in the proper adjuncts, in the course of time, passed into living organisms under the concurrence of God Who acted not as a Creator in the strict sense of the term, but as the provident governor and administrator of the things He had created "*movens deinde administransque per temporales cursus ea ipsa quae condidit.*" The charge is made by some writers at the present time that such an interpretation of the doctrine of Augustine is synonymous with modern evolution and that it makes an evolutionist of Augustine himself. Such utterances are bold, to say the least. I prefer to call the system of Augustine "virtualism."

When Augustine embraced the theory of the seminal reasons and proposed it as a solution of the difficulty involved in the simultaneous creation of all things in this world, he did not intend that it should be so circumscribed as to apply only to the order of things as they were known in his day, provided an extended application of this theory were possible. He accepted the theory in all its implications, on condition, however, that it be used in accordance with reason and Faith. This seems to square with his confession of partial failure (as he thought, and as was indicated in the Retractions) in the compilation of the work on Genesis.

Hence if the virtualism of Augustine avails us anything in the explanation of natural phenomena, it must be admitted that we are justified in accepting it for what it is worth. And I think that if the opinion was recognized in the past by great scholars as possessed of some probability, we are certainly warranted at the present time in looking upon it as very probable and most useful in explaining certain facts that are adduced by science, to which we may not close our eyes. For it is consonant with the recent theories of the geologists, paleontologists, yes, and with those of the physicists and biologists. What is more, it is also consistent with the opinions of the scholastics on the constitution of bodies, whether these be organic or inorganic. It enables us to propound solutions to the many difficulties that are proposed by the scientists; and under the guidance of the great Doctor we can arm ourselves with a ready answer to many questions that will be hurled at us in virtue of the newly-claimed discoveries that seem to be in the offing. I do not contend that the claims of the scientists will be established; I do not know. But I do claim that whatever is set before us as a fact categorically proved, or a deduction that logically flows from proven facts, will be susceptible of explanation in the light of the doctrine of the Bishop of Hippo. In the development of the questions that are to follow I shall endeavor to make clear my meaning.

By many it is maintained that the seminal reasons as referred to in the writings of Augustine are to be understood in a passive sense, at least to the extent that the passive potency of matter (the determinable element of bodies) even when it is determined by the seminal reasons, remains in a state of pure passivity; by the addition of the seminal reasons there is constituted an "obediential relation of receptivity to the creative word, with regard to the form of each individual to come into being by creation in its own time. That Saint Augustine in the treatise *De Trinitate* treats them in some way as active principles, implies no contradiction, since there he is not discussing creation, but is speaking of administration, and consequently views these seminal reasons not only as limitations of universal passive potency of matter, but also as in formed matter, active in the forms to which prime matter was by them determined." (Father Woods, *Augustine and Evolution*, p. 47.) As indicated above, it is the natural lot of man to differ with others in the interpretation of a text or document, with the result that conflicting views are propounded by both sides. The only remedy for this is the establishment of an authoritative tribunal capable of passing infallible judgment on the point at issue. We know that this matter is left to the free discussion of those who follow the teachings of Augustine, willing to accept what is firmly established; but we must also remember the guiding principle of the great Doctor: *"In dubiis libertas, in omnibus Caritas."* Since these motives impel all lovers of truth to investigate the latter and to follow the path of the light that directs us, treating with respect the views of those who do not agree with us, we shall continue to hold to the interpretation proposed by many leaders of thought in Catholic Theology who maintain that the seminal reasons are active.

It is well, however, to advert to the fact that Augustine draws a very clear and essential distinction between the seminal reasons of the natural order and the predispositions of nature to the supernatural effects of miracles and grace. For we hold that the seminal reasons are certain powers positively introduced by the Creator into the material world or created things, in order that by a necessary impulse they may evolve into those things intended by God. The supernatural predispositions, on the other hand, are not some positive entity inserted in things from the beginning, by which those things may, of themselves, function in the higher (supernatural) order, but they are merely passive potencies, by which created things are from the very beginning preordained to this, that God as the Administrator of the things He created, may do in these things and with these things what He deems fitting. This observation is necessary, lest we confound the two orders, and is warranted by the words quoted above (p. 34, last citation). Hence we conclude:

1. In the first formation of things, God produced in creation certain causal reasons or quasi-seminal reasons;

2. These seminal reasons were *active* potencies for the development of the natural order of creation and are to be distinguished from the passive potencies (obediential potentiality) by which God is able to act on them for the production of supernatural effects;

3. These powers do not exclude God but necessarily require that concurrence by which He exerts an influx

in all actions of creatures, in order that the proper effect may be wrought;

4. The influx of God on created things by which He produces supernatural effects is not contrary to nature, but, rather, perfective of nature in a higher sense; for He, in the establishment of nature, made it in such a way as to allow for these acts of intervention by which effects that transcend their natural powers are effected in them by the Creator. "It remains therefore," says Saint Augustine, "that created things were adapted to both modes: either to that by which temporal things run their course in the most accustomed manner, or to that by which rare and wonderful events occur, as it shall please God to do what is suitable to the time." (*Gen. ad. l.*, Book 6.) [1]

## II. Spontaneous Generation

In answer to the second question: "Is spontaneous generation consistent with Saint Augustine's views?" I think it well to direct attention to the different terminology used by Augustine and by ourselves. In addition to this it is necessary to recall what has been stated already, that this term is taken in an entirely different sense by the materialists and by those who are convinced that it may be understood in a sense entirely orthodox. The former, identical with abiogenesis, as explained above, is opposed to biogenesis. The term abiogenesis, first used by Huxley in 1870, is employed to designate the theory according to which living matter is assumed to derive its origin from non-living matter. This theory was looked upon as altogether disproved by the elaborate experiments made by Spallanzani, Pasteur and others. And even Huxley admitted that they had shown that the "doctrine of biogenesis, life from life, is victorious all along the line." But there is no doubt that further experiments are constantly being carried out with the express purpose of "creating" life in the laboratory.

Two recent writers from among Catholic scholars, Fathers O'Brien and Messenger, commenting upon this phase of the question, do not hesitate to assert that spontaneous generation must

[1] *Cf.* Del Val, *Theol. Dogmat. I De Deo creante.*

be accepted as an established fact and in accord with the explicit teaching of the great Fathers, as well as that of great scholastic theologians. Doctor Messenger, on page 16 of the work mentioned before, states "As a result of . . . examination of the Sacred Text, we conclude that Holy Scripture, according to its plain and obvious sense, definitely teaches the origin of all living things from inorganic matter, by what may well be called 'spontaneous generation.' The fact that this teaching is contained in Sacred Scripture can hardly, we think, be denied. And those who disbelieve in the possibility of spontaneous generation, even at the beginning of life on the earth, are forced to have recourse to hypotheses which seem to us hardly in harmony with the principle of the veracity of Sacred Scripture." (He then cites Janssens to the effect that the origin of living things from inorganic matter must be put under the heading of "elements of human knowledge," rather than among the "elements of revealed truth.") He concludes: "It is difficult to see how this is to be reconciled with the complete veracity of the Scriptures, and we prefer to hold that Scripture really teaches spontaneous generation, and that this must accordingly be accepted as true. Our position becomes much stronger when it is realized that it has the general support of the Fathers."

That conflicting interpretations of Scriptures and the Fathers are frequently made by students of these sources is brought home to us in so many instances, that they occasion no surprise, nor need they affect us seriously. We know that the Fathers of the Church are to be recognized as the authoritative interpreters (subject to the decision of the Church) of the Sacred Scriptures. But when we study their writings, we find it extremely difficult, at times, to determine whether they set forth their teachings as witnesses of revealed truth, or as private commentators. That Saint Augustine acted in the latter rôle, with regard to the *rationes seminales,* can hardly be questioned. Hence we may treat his views as those of a wise leader, and at the same time we must, in the spirit of charity which animated the Bishop of Hippo in his dealings with those who failed to agree with him, grant to those who reject Augustine's "virtualism," or our interpretation of it, the latitude and liberty we desire for ourselves.

Now, may virtualism as propounded by the great Doctor, be of such a character as to entail spontaneous generation, or, at least, to admit of such a theory? Considered from one point of view, I think we are justified in saying that spontaneous generation holds no place in the system of simultaneous and virtual creation. But it is well to bear in mind what was said above concerning the doctrine of virtualism. From a careful analysis of the work of Augustine in this respect, we are constrained to conclude that, to the mind of Augustine, the beginnings of life differed, in notable respects, from the beginnings as we apprehend them at the present time, as the result of the work of men of science. According to our view, the simplest element of life is the cell; and at the root of this,—the substratum, so to speak,— is brute matter. Hence in a living thing there are two principles: matter and a vital principle. In the system of Saint Augustine the most simple elements were the causal or seminal reasons of life, which were created directly by God from the beginning of time, together with the cosmic matter that constituted the material universe. By the creation of the seminal reasons, God created virtually, in the beginning, all the species of living things that were to appear in their full stage of perfection in the course of time. Augustine proposes this to us in all seriousness as his own concept of the origin of life in its beginnings. He looks upon the seminal reasons as real entities or powers. This is evident from the twenty-second chapter of the seventh book on Genesis: "We are forced to fear lest we be suspected of uttering senseless words when we say that God did not create those *very natures* and *substances* that were to appear, at the time in which He created all things at once (simul), but (we say) that He created certain causal reasons of those things that were to appear."

Now if we understand by spontaneous generation the production of a living thing,—for example, life in its lowest form,—from matter that is inanimate and exists before life is present in it in any way, I think we must conclude that Augustine did not admit spontaneous generation: for the *simultaneous* existence of the seminal reasons of life with the matter that was created in the beginning and which were implanted with matter by God, seems to exclude the antecedence of matter that is required for spontaneous generation. Since life in its causal reasons was made with matter it can hardly be said to come from matter as the exponents of abiogenesis maintain. But we must remember the different modes of conceiving this relation between brute matter and life, as indicated above. It appears that Augustine's seminal reasons were much more simple than are the constituents of things as we understand them now.

To us the simplest thing that may be considered in the life of a plant or animal is the cell. If we accept the theory of Laplace regarding the formation of the universe, we are forced to admit that an organism made up of these cells could not have lived during the periods preceeding the solidification and cooling process of the globe. Hence there must have been some definite time in which the first living things appeared upon the earth *"in actu,"* and this seems to bring us to the point where spontaneous generation is accepted as a postulate by many authorities who are unwilling to admit the intervention of God by creation. Regardless of how broad our views may be in aligning ourselves with the scientists, we know for certain that such an act of intervention on the part of the Creator is possible; and if no valid explanation were available, and if spontaneous generation, as the only alternative, were proved to be absurd and impossible, we should not hesitate to subscribe to direct creation, or its equivalent, as effected by the Author of all.

Reverting now to the consideration of the term we shall begin with the definition of "spontaneous" as given in Webster's New Dictionary (unabridged): Spontaneous—Proceeding from, or acting by, internal impulse, energy, or natural law, without external force." Although Webster's adverts to the fact that rigid interpretation of spontaneous generation is no longer held, I thing it well for the present purpose to assume, for the sake of clarity, that the definition submitted above, is susceptible of the interpretation placed upon it by the exponents of abiogenesis in its more material (or, materialistic) form. For this latter would be taken care of by the phrase "without external force." In fact this is what is intended by the abiogenists, and it is their purpose to exclude the action of God Who is viewed as an external force. But, taking for granted that God created all things and that He concurs in the actions of creatures, we ask whether the definition contained in the dictionary, including the phrase, "without external force," can be understood in such a manner as to be compatible with the system of virtualism proposed by Saint Augustine. I think it can. And to the extent that admission is made in this respect, I think spontaneous generation is conformable to the teachings of Augustine.

Considering the cell as the foundation of the organism, as explained by biologists, we see that, as a material entity, it is composed of many parts. Elsewhere we considered the view of Haldane, an authority in the field of Bio-Chemistry, that a cell contains over ten thousand, but less than a million, distinct chemical substances. Regardless of the number of elements or chemical substances contained in a cell, the fact is that definite elements of determined quality and proportion are assuredly required. This is all that concerns us for the development of the problem entrusted to us regarding the origin of life by what may be called spontaneous generation. It is clear that the latter term is to be taken in the sense of *production* rather than in the sense in which generation is frequently understood by scholars when they identify it with the origin of one living thing from another. For in the latter case there is no difficulty involved.

One of the most universal laws of which we are aware is the law of change in the material world. As the result of observation and rational interpretation, the old philosophers were able to formulate a principle that is commonly accepted by both philosophers and natural scientists: *"Corruptio unius, generatio alterius*—the corruption or dissolution of one thing involves the production of another thing." When, for example, in the labora-

tory the chemist unites two elements in proper proportions, something entirely distinct from the components is produced. This
phenomenon is not ascribable to a miracle; it is not creation in
the commonly accepted sense of that term. It is production,
or, as stated above, it is generation. It is not due to what we
ordinarily call some outside force, but is in accord with the
internal tendencies of the component parts. If the chemist is
capable of bringing about the conditions that are indispensable
to their union, we surely cannot deny to God, the Author of the
elements and their natural tendencies, the power to so arrange
His material world that at the proper time and in the proper adjuncts the law of union of the material elements that constitute an
organism shall apply to these components. I do not question
the most obvious truth, admitted by most Biologists, that life
cannot arise from mere brute matter; I do not believe that the
origin of life can be explained by the mere matter-and-motion-
evolution theory. But I do think that the elements that constitute an organism, although existing for ages in a quasi-inorganic
state, were from the very beginning possessed of the seminal
principles by which, in the course of time, they were to emerge as
organisms endowed with the corporeal life that was preordained
for them from the primordial existence of the world. How this
was accomplished is not for us to say. God knows how to do
things that are wholly beyond our ken. He tells us through
an inspired author that He has left the earth to men, to discover
what is hidden therein. And I think the scientists and those who
align themselves with the scientists are justified in attempting to
explain what can be explained by the light of reason, whether
this latter acts in accordance with its own principles, or in
harmony with, and under the guidance of principles derived from
a source that surpasses pure nature. There is no doubt that
many difficulties will confront us in this venture, but difficulties
will never make a lover of the truth waver in his allegiance to the
One Who contains in Himself the explanation of all mysteries,
natural as well as supernatural. Perhaps the greatest difficulty
in this connection is based upon what seems to be the emergence of

life from something that is inferior to life. But in the system of virtualism, which I have attempted to explain, such difficulty should not deter us, for the simple reason that life is accounted for by the causal reasons advanced by Saint Augustine which are ultimately referred to God. Even in our own day we have to admit that the nature of life in its lowest form is not clearly understood. We know that it does not proceed, in the lower organisms, from a spiritual principle. We know that it does not proceed from a principle that is capable of existing outside of matter; that it cannot function independently of matter; but we cannot define it in such a manner as to leave nothing to be desired. Some describe it as "a vital force," thereby distinguishing it from mechanical force and the like, and rest content with such a description. But the truth is that there are still many things to be explained regarding the nature of the lower forms. What I wish to insist upon principally is, that these lower forms cannot be placed in the same category as the form or soul of the human organism, and that it is possible for us to treat of them in their origin in a manner entirely different from that which holds true in the case of the spiritual soul. An act of creation as explained above is necessary in the latter instance. But such creation need not be postulated for the emergence of lower forms, provided we admit that all things, even the vegetative and animal soul derived their existence through creation of the seminal reasons in virtue of which they actually come into being. In conclusion, then, we feel justified in stating that the virtualism propounded by Saint Augustine does not entail spontaneous generation as advanced by the abiogenists, but that the term "spontaneous generation" as explained above, is in full accord with the doctrine of the Bishop of Hippo.

### III. Transformation of Species

In answer to the third question "May we, under the leadership of Saint Augustine, admit the transformation of species?" it is necessary to state at the very outset that this theory never occurred to the Holy Doctor. The only way in which we may admit that it has any bearing upon the doctrine of virtualism is by implication, in so far as the principles of virtual creation may be applied to the facts known to us. In the explanation of species already given in this article, I endeavored to state the question in accordance with facts with which we are acquainted. Acting under the influence of scientists and guided by principles of philosophy employed by such able thinkers as Doctor Albert Farges and others of the later school of Scholastic Philosophy, I expressed my opinion regarding a definite degree of fixity or constancy of species. At no time did I lose sight of the recent theory that all the species of today come to us by progressive development from one or a few primitive types. Here we have a recurrence of the old difficulty: various interpretations derived from the same "text"; in this case the text is the book of nature, continually unfolded to our gaze, thanks to the labors of the men of science. It may be that in the concluding pages of this vast book scientists and philosophers of succeeding ages will discover the rules by which the entire book is to be interpreted. Since I am not aware of the existence of a different "key" I think interpreters are warranted in their assertion that we must try to interpret nature by the application of norms known to us at the present time.

My firm conviction is that this procedure was at the root of Saint Augustine's explanation of the origin of things. His genius as a philosopher enabled him to advance the principles which he proposed and which he set forth for the acceptance of those to whom they seemed probable.

All theistic supporters of modern evolution defend this theory because of the discoveries of the scientists; Saint Augustine was not possessed of this knowledge and we should be rash were we to deduce from his teachings the extravagant conclusion that he upheld evolution as we know it now. But this does not mean that he may be considered an opponent of evolution. That he did not teach genetic descent of all things from a single, or from a few original progenitors, I am firmly convinced. That he did not ascribe all the members of a given species to a single progenitor (plant or animal) is, likewise, I think, to be admitted. For, in Sermon 268, No. 3 (Ed. Migne) he states:

> Unity is commended in the creation of things and in the birth of Christ. Most beloved, God highly recommends unity. Let this have some influence on you, that in the beginning of creation (creatures), when God founded all things, when He made the stars in heaven, and herbs and trees on the earth, He said: let the earth bring forth, and the trees and all green things were produced; He said: let the waters bring forth swimming creatures and things that fly, and it was so done. Did God make the other birds from one bird? Did He make all fishes from one fish? All horses from one horse? All the beasts from one beast? Did not the earth produce many things at once (simul), and bring to perfection many things by (means of) many fetuses? The moment came for the formation of man *(ventum est ad hominem faciendum)* and one man was made, the human race from one man. He did not wish to make two separately, male and female: but one, the man, and from the one man (He made) one woman *(Sed unum, et de uno unam)*. Why did God act thus? Why is the human race sprung (inchoatur) from one man, unless it be that unity is recommended to the human race?

From this citation it seems quite obvious that the theory of evolution was unknown to Augustine and that he interpreted scripture in accordance with the facts as they were known in his day. We are hardly justified, however, in concluding that it was the intention of the Doctor to refute antecedently the claims that were to be made in our day. Augustine gives not the slightest intimation that he is speaking as a witness of any revelation that had been made regarding the interpretation of these words. He takes the words in what he deems the obvious sense, influenced, no doubt, by the scientific opinions then current.

But admitting, at least for the sake of clearing up the question, that Augustine did not incline to evolution as a fact, may we admit that his theory of virtualism is consistent with evolution, at least in some form? My personal view is that the system of

Augustine as accepted and explained elsewhere *is* applicable to evolution of species in some way. It is not my desire, and certainly not my duty, to restrict the application of the principles of virtualism to the limits I indicated when I treated of the stability of species. I discussed the stability of species from the viewpoint of fact and legitimate deduction. If Augustine's positive and actual stand did not involve the teaching of evolution in its more moderate form, and is reconcilable with evolution as many are inclined to accept it, as outlined in the development of species, I firmly believe that it will be just as consistent with the more extreme forms of evolution if they are substantiated in the future, provided they accept the influx of God upon nature, as the Creator and Administrator thereof. It seems probable that the theory of virtualism, just as it was shown to be in accord with the origin and development of life in the individual, is, also, in accord with the development of the species. How far the limits extend is not for me to state, but for savants in the field of science to prove.

Perhaps a momentary consideration of the development of species as set forth by those in a position to speak will throw more light upon my meaning. There are many heads under which the general argument might be built up, but I confine myself to the consideration of only a few. In fact, support for evolution is drawn from Genetics, Serology, Taxonomy, Embryology, Morphology, Selection, Paleontology, Geographical distribution, etc. I shall consider only the last five.

1. The embryos of the higher animals develop gradually from a lower to a higher stage of perfection passing through various forms and in a definite order. It was the common view of Scholastics that there appeared first the vegetative soul or form, and this was succeeded, in due time, by the higher or sentient soul. What is true of the individual can be true also of the species, with the natural consequence that in the course of time the species ascend from a lower to a higher degree of perfection. And just as the embryo contains in itself, virtually, at the beginning of its existence, all the perfection that it will manifest

in the course of its development, so also may the original types have contained virtually in themselves the ultimate perfections that were to be acquired only after many generations.

2. The next argument is based upon the form and structure of plants and animals. Zoologists inform us that in the animal kingdom there are found certain main types characterizing the principal divisions of this kingdom, which seem to indicate the fact that all the members of the respective groups are fashioned in accordance with a general design that runs through the entire division. Although some differences of structure are found in the later groups, there is very good reason to assume that they all descended from common progenitors. Since the differences are accounted for with comparative ease, or, at least with a degree of probability that borders on conviction, the arguments against this explanation are effectively refuted.

3. It is an established fact that specialists in their respective fields are able to effect variations in living things which are most remarkable; by crossing they are able to bring about what seem to be new species, and, by many, are styled such. If this is true in our day when the species have arrived, perhaps, at the point of full development, we are justified in admitting that these and even greater results could have been accomplished in the ages past when the species were, perhaps, more pliable.

4. Many Paleontologists assure us that there can be no doubt that in time the less perfect organisms preceded the more perfect. Examining the strata of the earth they have clear evidence to the effect that in the successive epochs of the earth's history there is continual gradation and thereby conclude that the more perfect were descended from those that preceded them.

5. The last argument is based upon the differences among plants and animals that live in different parts of the world. The claim is made that the respective environment—means, circumstances, etc.—is responsible for developments that are peculiar to the place in which they are found; from which it is deduced that external adjuncts play a very important and determining part in the formation of the species.

By way of comment on the foregoing I may remark that many notable differences in organisms can be reasonably explained by the principles of transformism. This is true even of the human race, which is said to have originated in the last or quarternary epoch. Hence we cannot sensibly exclude from the lower orders factors that have accomplished such changes in man. We have every reason to admit that these agencies account for the development of systematic species, but not the same cogent reasons for admitting the transit of natural or fundamental species to one of a higher order. It is more difficult to assent to those who claim that the animal kingdom proceeded from the vegetable kingdom. In this connection I may say that there are many who restrict evolution of species to a few types in each order. Just how far one may go in accordance with the findings of science is not a matter upon which all transformists of what is styled the "moderate school" agree. But I do not hesitate to advance the opinion that any degree of evolution that is verified will be conformable to the fundamental principle of virtualism proposed by Saint Augustine. For he tells us very definitely that "God created all terrestrial animals as the last denizens from the last element (that was formed); but only potentially, whose numbers time was to unfold later so as to render them visible (visibiliter)." (De Gen. ad Litt., V, 14.)

He did not say how they were to be unfolded for he had no means of acquiring this information. Apparently he did not suspect such genetic relation as is now proposed by the evolutionists; but this was because he had not the facts upon which to base an opinion regarding the actual appearance of things upon the earth in the visible manner to which he alludes. Although Saint Augustine thought it a fact that not all the animals were genetically related, although he did not adhere to such a relation in the vegetable kingdom, as appears from the citation from Sermon 268, given above, still he was convinced of the general principle of virtual development by reason of the seminal causes. If, in commenting upon individual facts such as those just cited, he speaks in such a manner that his opinion seems to exclude the rigorous application of the principle of virtualism, it was merely because he had no reason to suspect such a relation as even the moderate transformists are now willing to admit. Augustine does not touch directly upon the question whether living things appeared upon the earth in act in a rather perfect state of development or in consequence of a slow evolution, but his manner of treatment seems to indicate that he favored the latter in preference to the former from a speculative point of view. And if this be true with regard to the individual, it certainly is not opposed to the principles of virtualism to apply them to the development of the sensible organic type. That is, just as a plant or animal now passes through various stages in its development from the embryo to its full growth, so also could the species have passed through various stages in attaining its full development in accordance with the determination imparted to the seminal reasons when they were created. To Augustine it is a matter of indifference whether the seed came first or the complete living plant or animal, for he says in this connection: *(De Gen. ad Litt.,* V, 23), "It can be admitted that it is uncertain whether seeds proceeded from animals, or animals from seeds; but whichever came first, it is most certain that the (original ones) came from the earth." If Augustine were certain that the first animals or plants (or the seeds of same) were formed directly by God in a complete rather than in a potential form, I feel confident that he would have apprised us of his conviction on this score. But from his writings we have very good reason to believe the contrary. Even such a conservative philosopher as Albert Farges, who cannot be accused of biased leanings to evolution admits that the virtualism of Augustine is applicable to the theory of transformism.

\*     \*     \*     \*     \*

Thus we have been led gradually to the consideration of evolution in its last phase: the formation of man from some pre-existing organism. By many the answer to the question regarding the origin and formation of man is sought in the most trustworthy of ancient documents, the Sacred Scriptures. As might be expected, some have labored under the impression that the theory of evolution in all its forms had been antecedently condemned by revelation; others are of the opinion that solid support for the theory is derived from the sacred pages. Here again we are confronted with the old difficulty: different interpretations from the same text.

A careful appraisal of the two extremes constrains us to say that both statements are exaggerated, for the simple reason that Moses, having in view merely the religious and moral good of the people whom he guided, laid aside all preoccupation of the various genera and species, in their philosophical or scientific sense. There can be no doubt that these questions have been left by God and the author of Genesis to the free discussion of men. Both rival opinions are reconcilable with Genesis; not, of course, that both opinions can be true, but no matter which one is proved to conform to facts, the words of Scripture will not lose the meaning intended by the Sacred Author. It is the task of capable investigators to find out the true sense of Holy Writ, not the duty of Moses to teach us truths of the merely natural order. But though conflicting opinions may be held by the members of opposing schools of thought, it is necessary to remember that in these domestic questions one may not brand the other with any stigma. The Church alone is authorized to pass definitive judgment, and, until she speaks, full liberty is to hold sway in matters that are not clear. However, it does not require keen insight to apprehend how untenable are the extremes to which many zealots go. Recently we witnessed the humiliating spectacle of Evolution being legislated out of the classroom. This form of bias, which maintains that evolution is formally condemned by the Bible is far more reprehensible than that which contends that it is taught by the Bible. We know that the attacks made upon evolution on the authority of the Bible have been responsible in great measure for the opinion among many educated but misguided persons: that the ultimate proof of evolution would sound the death knell of the spirituality of the soul, of the existence of God, of the inspiration of the Sacred Scriptures, of the immortality of the spiritual man, etc. When the day arrives on which we shall be able to make all concerned realize that the theory of evolution, even though it be transformed into a thesis, cannot affect the place God occupies in the world, that it cannot redound to the detriment of, or, a fortiori, to the destruction of religion, morality or immortality, on that day unrestrained and unreflecting enthusiasm for these new discoveries or novelties will be tempered.

## Authority and Teaching of Sacred Scripture

Since the Bible is so often quoted to substantiate the claims of the anti-evolutionists as well as to bolster up the contentions of the transformists, it will be conducive to the proper treatment of this question to consider the attitude we must assume with regard to several very important truths intimately connected with evolution and related to the inspired Text. For the sake of brevity I shall consider only those factors which are immediately connected with the matter under discussion, and shall treat of them under four heads:

1. Revelation contained in Sacred Scripture.

2. The authority of the Fathers in their interpretation of the Sacred Text.

3. The influence of science upon the interpretation of Sacred Scripture.

4. The origin of man as taught by Sacred Scripture.

### 1. Revelation Contained in Sacred Scripture

Pope Leo XIII in his famous Encyclical "Providentissimus Deus" describes succinctly the conviction of the Church throughout the ages that "Supernatural revelation, according to the belief of the universal Church, is contained both in unwritten tradition and in written books, which are, therefore, called sacred and canonical because, "being written under the inspiration of the Holy Ghost, they have God for their Author, and as such have been delivered to the Church." This belief has been perpetually held and professed by the Church in regard to the books of both Testaments" . . . All the books which the Church receives as sacred and canonical are written wholly and entirely, with all their parts, at the dictation of the Holy Ghost; and so far is it from being possible that any error can co-exist with inspiration, that inspiration not only is essentially incompatible with error, but excludes and rejects it as absolutely and necessarily as it is impossible that God Himself, the Supreme truth, can utter that which is not true. This is the ancient and unchanging faith of the Church. . . . And the Church holds the canonical books as sacred not because, having been composed by human industry, they were afterwards approved by her authority, nor only because they contain revelation without error, but because, having been written under the inspiration of the Holy Ghost, they have God for their Author. Hence, because the Holy Ghost employed men as His instruments, we cannot say that it was these inspired instruments who, perchance, have fallen into error, and not the primary Author. For, by supernatural power He so moved and impelled them to write, He was so present to them that the things which He ordered, and those only, they, first, rightly understood, then willed faithfully to write down, and finally expressed in apt words and with infallible truth . . . it follows that those who maintain that an error is possible in any genuine passage of the sacred writings either pervert the Catholic notion of inspiration or make God the Author of such error. And so emphatically were all the Fathers and Doctors agreed that the divine writings, as left by the hagiographers, are free from all error, that they labored earnestly, with no less skill than reverence, to reconcile with each other those numerous passages which seem at variance. The words of Saint Augustine to Saint Jerome sum up what the Fathers taught: "On my own part I confess to your charity that it is only to those books of scripture which are now called canonical that I have learned to pay such honor and reverence as to believe most firmly that none of their writers has fallen into any error. And if in these books I meet anything which seems contrary to truth, I shall not hesitate to conclude either that the text is faulty, or that the translator has not expressed the meaning of the passage, or that I myself do not understand." (Ep. 82.)

All exegetes and theologians teach that inspiration, of itself, prescinds from revelation. It is true that many things written down by the human Author could be derived only from revelation (such as mysteries not before declared, prophecies, etc.) but it is just as true that many descriptions contained in the Bible were rendered possible by the industry of the inspired Author. Likewise, inspiration does not influence the style or literary methods of the writer, but merely the portrayal of the truth intended by the Holy Ghost. With regard to us, however, the beneficiaries of the books written by the inspired Authors, the Bible in its entire content is assuredly to be accepted as the revealed word of God to teach us. "All Scripture," says Saint Paul, "inspired of God, is profitable to *teach,* to reprove, to correct, to instruct in justice, that the man of God may be perfect, furnished to every good work." (2 Tim. 3:16-17.)

The revealed truths taught us by Holy Writ may be divided into two general groups: First, those which are principally or directly intended by God, and secondly, those which constitute the indirect, secondary or concomitant object of revelation. In the first category we have (a) all those truths which pertain exclusively to the supernatural order, such as the mysteries contained in the symbol of faith with all that logically derives therefrom; (b) certain truths of the natural order which are indispensable to the higher order, such as the spirituality and the immortality of the human soul, etc. In the second group we have the remaining truths of revelation which, although intended by God for our instruction or edification, do not constitute the object primarily intended by Him; such are, for example (a) many historical facts which are accidentally connected with those of the supernal order; (b) certain natural phenomena which are accidentally connected with revealed truths of the supernatural order, such as the statements found in Genesis pertaining to the formation of the world, which are concomitantly

...led with the fundamental and more important truth that ...d is the Author and Creator of all things.

With regard to the truths of the first category, it is the universal teaching of Exegetes and Theologians that it is the primary intention of God, Who inspired the Hagiographers, to teach religious truths by means of the inspired book; that the principal purpose of Inspiration was to have man believe in God as He is manifested in the Sacred Scriptures and to have him seek his Creator by means of them. Saint Augustine, in his Confessions says: "Since we were too weak by abstract reasonings to find out the truth and for this very cause needed the authority of Holy Writ; I had now begun to believe, that Thou wouldst never have given such excellent authority to that Scripture in all lands, hadst Thou not willed thereby to be believed in and by It to be sought. For now that things, sounding strangely in the Scripture, were wont to offend me, having heard divers of them expounded satisfactorily, I referred to the depth of the mysteries, and its authority appeared to me the more venerable and more worthy of religious credence, in that, while it lay open to all to read, it reserved the majesty of its mysteries within its profounder meaning, stooping to all in the great plainness of its words and lowliness of its style, yet calling forth the intensest application of such as are not light of heart." (*Conf. B.*, 6, Chap. V, 8.). It was not the set purpose of the Author of the Bible to teach men profane sciences, such as astronomy, zoology, geology, and so forth. For this reason we must admit that the Scriptures, in so far as they make known the truths that are necessary for salvation, are to be considered in a class by themselves and are to be interpreted in accordance with norms that are derived from a higher source than those subject to reason alone. Hence the sciences based upon natural reason can play only a negative part in determining the sense of Sacred Scripture in these matters: that is, by reason we are able to exclude all interpretations that border on the absurd and by it we are able to present the doctrine of revelation in such a manner as to make our assent to revelation highly reasonable. In fact we know that by means of the revealed

teachings of Holy Scripture we have been able to refine philosophical thought, as may be seen from a consideration of the
true sense of the terms used in connection with the Blessed
Trinity, the Hypostatic Union, etc.

However, in those matters that do not constitute the principal
object of revelation, when the sense of the sacred text is not clear,
it is not only lawful, but necessary to have recourse to the
principles of science and to positive historical facts, in order
to determine the sense of the inspired text. This method or procedure has been adopted by the Fathers and the great Doctors
throughout the ages, and we cannot deny this privilege to sincere
scholars of our time. Saint Thomas is very clear on this point,
and he proposes to us a norm of action that may be adopted as
a safe guide. Having distinguished between those things that
pertain to the deposit of faith either directly (*per se*) or indirectly
(*per accidens*) he touches upon the origin of the world, and
states: "With regard to the origin (*principium*) of the world
there is something that pertains to the substance of faith, namely,
that the world had its beginning by creation, and on this all
the Saints are agreed. But the *manner* and *order* in which the
world was made does not pertain to faith except indirectly (*per
accidens*), in so far as it is related in Scripture, which truth
the Saints have safeguarded although they have rendered different explanations thereof." (*In.* 2, d. 12, a. 2.) Hence in
matters that pertain to the natural sciences, we are justified
in attempting to determine the sense of Sacred Scripture by
means of scientific principles and we should not appeal to the
scripture as to a textbook on natural science. Laws which are
scientifically established today must be accepted as having been
effective in the beginning. There is no valid reason for our
assuming otherwise. "Scripture," says Saint Thomas, "in the first
part of Genesis makes mention of the institution of nature which
thence continues. Hence we should not say that something took
place then which did not continue thereafter." For this reason
we conclude with the same Doctor that "in the first establishment of nature we may not look for a miracle, but for what
accords with the nature of things." (I, q. 67, a. 3.)

## 2. Authority of the Fathers in Their Interpretation of Scripture

By the Fathers we mean those noble champions of the Faith, who, living in the early centuries of the Church, were renowned for their orthodox doctrine and sanctity of life, and have been approved by the Church as exponents of the truths revealed to us by God. Although scholars versed in Patrology do not agree on the exact date on which the Patristic era came to a close, it is commonly admitted that the last of the Greek Fathers was Saint John Damascene who died about 754, and the last of the Fathers of the Latin Church was Saint Isidore of Seville, who died in 636. For practical purposes we shall rest content with the opinion of the majority.

That we have need of guides in the interpretation of the Bible is a fact so obvious that it cannot be reasonably questioned. For as Saint Augustine rightly remarks: "If there is no branch of learning however humble and easy to learn, which does not require a master, what can be a greater sign of rashness and pride than to refuse to study the books of the divine mysteries by the help of those who have interpreted them." (*Ad Honorat.*) The other Fathers have said the same, and have confirmed it by their example, for they "endeavored to acquire the understanding of the Holy Scriptures not by their own lights and ideas but from the writing and authority of the ancients, who, in their turn, as we know, received the rule of interpretation in direct line from the Apostles." (Rufinus, Hist. Eccl. *Cf.* Encycl. Prov. Deus.) Pope Leo XIII, in the celebrated Encyclical referred to, tells us that "The Holy Fathers are of supreme authority, whenever they all interpret in one and the same manner any text of the Bible, as pertaining to the *doctrines of Faith and morals;* for their unanimity clearly evinces that such interpretation has come down from the Apostles as a matter of Catholic faith. The opinion of the Fathers is also of very great weight when they treat of these matters in their capacity of Doctors unofficially; not only because they excel in their knowledge of revealed doctrine and in their acquaintance with many things which are useful in understanding the apostolic books, but because they are men of eminent sanctity and of ardent zeal for the truth, on whom God has bestowed a more ample measure of His light. Wherefore the expositor should make it his duty to follow their footsteps with all reverence, and to use their labors with intelligent appreciation." But when the Supreme Pontiff urges us to follow in the footsteps of the Fathers, it is not a command to accept everything that has been taught by the Fathers as private Doctors, for the simple reason that they propounded views, at times, which they had no intention of passing on to us as the interpretation of the revealed word of God handed down to them in authoritative teachings. If, as we have already seen, Sacred Scripture is divinely ordained, principally, to manifest those truths which are necessary for salvation, and on this score we are permitted great latitude in the interpretation of the sacred text in other matters, it stands to reason that a certain amount of liberty is accorded us in the interpretation of the works of the Fathers. Perhaps my meaning will be made clearer by contrast. Saint Thomas in his *Summa* (2, 2, q. 176, A. 1) says: "The Apostles were sufficiently instructed in wisdom and knowledge with regard to what the doctrine of faith required, but not with regard to all those things which are known through acquired science, as, for example, deductions drawn from arithmetic, or geometry." Certainly Saint Thomas has in mind the limitations of the Apostles in matters that involve the experimental sciences, particularly those that were to be developed at a later day. And if this be true of the Apostles, we are justified in assuming the same regarding the Fathers. For at no time do they boast of infused knowledge, nor do they arrogate to themselves revelation in fields that are not necessarily connected with the higher order. If they set forth their views in matters of a scientific character they do not propose them as the teachings of the Church. In fact they do not hesitate to reprove those who endeavor to use the Scriptures in support of opinions that are not propounded by Holy Writ. Let us consider the attitude of Augustine in this respect: "It is customary to inquire into the form and figure of heaven as proposed to us as a matter of belief according to our Scriptures.

Many have entered into long discussions concerning these things, which our Authors with greater prudence have omitted, since they are not profitable to the attainment of the blessed life . . . it must be stated briefly that the Spirit of God, who spoke through them (the Sacred Authors) did not wish to teach these things to men, as they are not profitable to salvation." (*De Gen.*, Book 2, chapter 9, 20.) The expressions that incidentally occur with reference to these scientific matters must be considered in the light of the knowledge that prevailed at the time in which the inspired authors wrote, and we know that at times the expressions used are those ordinarily employed by the untutored people, and at times are of a poetic character. And the same is true, at least in part, with regard to the writings of the Fathers. This is set forth admirably by the great Pontiff, Leo XIII (*Enc. Prov. Deus*): "The unshrinking defense of the Holy Scriptures, however, does not require that we should equally uphold all the opinions which each of the Fathers or the more recent interpreters have put forth in explaining them; for it may be that, in commenting upon passages where physical matters occur, they have sometimes expressed the ideas of their own times, and thus made statements which in these days have been abandoned as incorrect. Hence in their interpretations, we must carefully note what they lay down as belonging to the faith, or as intimately connected with faith—in what they are unanimous . . . Saint Thomas says most admirably: "When Philosophers are agreed upon a point, and it is not contrary to our faith, it is safer, in my opinion, neither to lay down such a point as a dogma of faith, even though it is perhaps so presented by the Philosophers, nor to reject it as against faith, lest we thus give to the wise of this world an occasion of despising our faith." The Catholic interpreter, although he should show that those facts of natural science which investigators affirm to be now quite certain are not contrary to the Scriptures rightly explained, must, nevertheless, always bear in mind that much which has been held and proved as certain has afterwards been called into question and rejected.

It is unfortunate that so many of our scholars in days gone by failed to act in accordance with this prudent norm so beautifully outlined by Pope Leo. It certainly may not be considered a new rule of direction, for repeatedly Saint Augustine and other great Fathers and Doctors of the Church counseled prudence and care. In the fifth century the former warned his followers "not to make rash assertions, or to assert what is not known as known." He pointed out a way for the adjustment of conflicts when he said "Whatever they (scientists) can really demonstrate to be true of physical nature we must show to be capable of reconciliation with our Scriptures." He said this because he knew that the Author of the Bible, the Holy Ghost, could not reveal anything that would at a later date conflict with the objective truths of science and although the Hagiographers were accustomed to deal with things in more or less figurative language, or in terms which were commonly used at the time, (and which in many instances are in daily use at this day, even by the most eminent men of science), the holy Doctor was firmly convinced that a proper mode of reconciliation could be proposed regardless of the findings of the sciences.

In conclusion, then, the Fathers, as witnesses of the truth revealed to the Church, are certainly infallible when considered morally unanimous on doctrines that pertain to the substance of Faith and Morals; in other matters, their teachings are subject to modification in accordance with the limits laid down in the exposition just submitted. We know that their views on many scientific matters have been rejected on the strength of discoveries made after their time. And if we consider evolution a problem for the scientists, we can just as well admit the right of departing from the views expressed in the writings of the Fathers, provided a substantial proof of the new claim be advanced. Obviously this statement is made with the reservations that have been proposed in respect to the fundamentals of our Holy Faith.

### 3. The Influence of Science Upon the Interpretation of Sacred Scripture

Saint Augustine, in his commentary on Genesis gives a very simple rule that should influence every tyro as well as every expert who attempts to express his views concerning the meaning of scriptural texts: "We must be on our guard against giving interpretations which are hazardous or opposed to science, and so exposing the word of God to the ridicule of unbelievers." From the time of the greatest thinkers of the patristic era, including such intellectual giants as Clement of Alexandria, Origen, Saint Athanasius, Saint Gregory of Nyssa, Saint Augustine, Saint Hilary, etc., there have not been lacking explanations of the first three chapters of Genesis, by which the Sacred text may be understood in such a manner as to preclude any possible conflict with the findings of the scientists. Even in our own day there are many who accept these traditional expositions, with some modifications, of course, as entirely satisfactory, and thereby show that there can never be any question of conflict between Revelation and the sciences. The limits of this article will not allow me to go into these theories in detail, or even *per summa capita*, but the explanations can easily be found in any handbook on Theology or Scripture. The Catholic Encyclopedia may be consulted with profit under the article "Hexaëmeron."

Although it is a fact that since the time of Darwin many, under the cloak of science, have endeavored to point out the untenability of the teachings of Sacred Scripture, because of the alleged incompatibility with the discoveries unearthed in recent years and the so-called logical deductions drawn therefrom, nevertheless this is not the attitude of the more conservative group of scientists as is evident from the pronouncements made by such eminent scholars as Professors Millikan, Campbell, Conklin, etc. We hold no brief for the scholars who have gone to the extreme of asserting that Genesis cannot be reconciled with science, but we must admit that their opinions have been based upon the unreasonable utterances of those who, posing as interpreters of Holy

Writ, have, without any warrant, resorted to the Bible as a text-book on the formation of the universe and the appearance of life upon the earth. Although refusing to condone those who view the Holy Scriptures as a textbook of science, we are constrained to refute those who go to the opposite extreme and assert that the revealed word or the teachings and practices of sound Religion serve as a detriment to the progress of the sciences. The attitude of the Catholic Church, attested by History, is succinctly stated by Leo XIII: "It is far, indeed, from our intention," he says in his letter to Cardinal Gibbons, January 22, 1899, "to repudiate all that the genius of the time begets; nay, rather, whatever the search for truth attains, or the effort after good achieves, will always be welcomed by Us, for it increases the patrimony of doctrine and enlarges the limits of public prosperity." If we glance at the achievements that mark the labors of Catholic Scholars in all fields of human learning, we shall see that the Faith which they held and still hold, has never deterred them from exploring the unknown in quest of the truth that is continuously being revealed to us by their investigations.

It must be remembered that when we were first introduced to these branches of knowledge certain definitions were laid down and we were assured that they squared with the truth as it was admitted by the scientists themselves; for example, that science, to use the definition given by Sir W. Hamilton, was viewed as "a complement of cognitions, having, in point of form, the character of logical perfection, and in point of matter, the character of real truth." When the scientist presents to us a real truth and deduces therefrom in a logical manner conclusions rightly warranted, we may not refuse our assent. But when they construct upon one or a few facts a theory which does not involve such logical perfection, we refuse to accept such deductions as strictly scientific. The claim may be viewed as a hypothesis or theory, and as such may be instrumental in leading us to a firm conviction regarding the objective truth, but until it has been conclusively demonstrated, it may not be foisted upon the world as a fact or real principle. The distinction between theory and established fact or principle is very clear, and the terms should not be used indiscriminately. To confuse them indicates a lack of scientific precision which should find no place in works of accredited scientists.

In concluding this point we assert with all Catholic theologians and exegetes that truths discovered by science must be accepted as valid norms for the interpretation of Sacred Scripture in those parts wherein scientific data are alluded to; and we unhesitatingly aver that there can be no danger of conflict since, in the last analysis, truths of the natural and supernatural orders derive their origin from the Author of all truth Who cannot contradict Himself.

#### 4. The Origin of Man As Taught in Sacred Scripture

Saint Augustine (Tr. in Joan, XVIII) tells us that "Heresies do not arise nor are there brought into being perverse doctrines which ensnare souls and cast them down into the depths, except when the good Scriptures are not well understood and when that is asserted with temerity and boldness which is not understood." No exegete could speak with greater authority on this point than the great Doctor who engaged in many controversies with erring scholars who foisted their erroneous interpretations of Scripture upon the unwitting followers who imbibed the poison of heresy served them. If we read the commentaries of Augustine on the meaning of the first chapters of Genesis we shall see how cautiously and with what great reserve this Doctor proposed his views. He never lost sight of the fact that mysterious meanings hidden beneath the obvious sense of the words of Genesis might be contained in the revelation accorded us by Moses; and for this reason he never insisted upon his own reasoned opinion being accepted unless it were supported by incontestable proof from other parts of Scripture or from some extrinsic authority. Even when he accepted as his own the view commonly prevailing among the leaders of the Church, he frequently proposed other explanations that seemed plausible and susceptible of proof at a later date. Thus at the present time the "theories" set forth by Augustine are receiving the recognition of scholars, and what seemed at one time fantastic is now becoming accepted as in accordance with the findings of modern science.

Unless there be a valid reason to proceed differently, it is a rule of hermeneutics that the words of any document be interpreted according to the obvious sense. This norm is applicable to Sacred Scripture. Guided by this principle many, in the days gone by—I should say the vast majority—were accustomed to take the words of the Bible, wherein reference is made to the origin of Man, as meaning that God formed him immediately from the slime of the earth. I refer, of course, to the body of the first man. There are several places in Holy Writ where mention is made of the formation of Adam's body. In Genesis, Chap. 11, v. 7 (following the Hebrew Text): "And the Lord God formed the man dust out of the earth and breathed into his nostrils the breath of life and the man became a living breath (creature)." Regarding the formation of Eve we read (Chap. 11, vv. 20-22): "But for the man there was not found a help like to him. And the Lord God caused a deep sleep to fall upon the man, and he slept; and He took one of his ribs (?) and closed up the flesh instead of it. And the rib, which the Lord God had taken from the man, He built into a woman and brought her to the man." Contrasting verse 7 with verse 19 of the same text: "And out of the earth the Lord God formed every beast of the field and every fowl of the air," many concluded that the Sacred Text eliminated the hypothesis of those who claim that Adam's body was derived from another animal, and asserted that the formation of the first man is to be ascribed exclusively to the direct action of God who used the slime of the earth as the material whence the body was formed. These same scholars maintain that the meaning of the Bible is clear from what is stated therein concerning Eve's origin. For there seems to be no valid reason based on consistency to ascribe the "descent" of Adam to the intermediary agency of lower animals, and deny such origin to Adam's helpmate. And there can be no doubt at all concerning Eve's dependence upon the body of Adam.

In Genesis III, 19, we read: "In the sweat of thy face shalt thou eat bread till thou return to the earth, out of which thou wast taken; for dust thou art, and into dust thou shalt return" (Vulgate). Solomon, in the Book of Ecclesiastes, XII, 7, says: "And the dust return into its earth from whence it was, and the spirit return to God Who gave it." The Author of the Book of Wisdom writes, VII, 1: "I myself also am a mortal man, like all others, and of the race of him that was first made of the earth." In Ecclesiasticus, XVII, 1: "God created man of the earth," and in Chap. XXXIII, 10: "And all men are from the ground, and out of the earth, from whence Adam was created." Tobias testifies, Chap. VIII, v. 8: "Thou madest Adam of the slime of the earth, and gavest him Eve for a helper."

Other texts may be cited to corroborate what is contained in the few transcribed above. The question proposed has to do with the interpretation of these testimonies. Do they connote the direct, immediate action of God, by which, without the intervening material frame of some lower animal, the body of Adam was formed? Until recent years it was thus commonly taught, by Catholics and Protestants alike. But at the present time such unanimity does not prevail. The number of "Christian Naturalists," as the exponents of the new doctrine are called, seems to be constantly growing. They assert that the words of Scripture are literally true even though God's action should be mediate, in so far as He works through the laws of nature established by Him. They cite Saint Thomas who teaches that: "What can be done by created power, need not be produced immediately by God" (*S. Theol.*, I, q. 91, art. 2). Indeed the more moderate among the Catholic Evolutionists postulate the direct action of the Creator in the formation of the first man from a lower organism. From the exegetical point of view it would seem that no fault could be found with this teaching. I mean this in the sense that the words of Scripture are susceptible of such a rendering, and are compatible with the conclusions drawn from the works of the scientists who have specialized in this field. I think no Exegete or Theologian of note will deny the possibility of all that is claimed by these Christian Naturalists. But the question is: do these claims square with the meaning intended by the Holy Ghost? We know that *"a posse ad esse non valet illatio"* and that which interests us in the present juncture is the fact, or manner in which man actually was formed. Since *"facta factis compro-bantur"* it is imperative that we appeal to those sources whence we derive our knowledge of the facts revealed to us in the inspired document. It is obvious that we are here alluding to those parts of the Bible that are not so clearly presented as to eliminate all danger of misunderstanding. In treating of these questions that are connected with our Holy Faith, it is necessary to keep before our minds the rules laid down by the only Authoritative Teacher, the Church. Sacred Scripture may seem very clear to us in many instances, but we know from experience that the most obvious sense is not always the true sense. Saint Peter warned the early Christians on this point, and we know that the Fathers, especially Saint Augustine, were always on their guard against attaching any sense to the words of Holy Writ that may be at variance with the one expounded by the Church. At all times the distinction has been made between the truths that are directly revealed by God and are intended for our direction in the spiritual life, and those that are revealed concomitantly and have no direct and necessary bearing upon our religious practices. With regard to the former, the Council of Trent speaks very clearly when it states (Session IV): "In order to restrain petulant spirits, IT (the Council) decrees, that no one, relying on his own skill, shall—*in matters of Faith and Morals pertaining to the edification of Christian doctrine*—wresting the Sacred Scripture to his own senses, presume to interpret the said Sacred Scripture contrary to that sense which holy Mother Church, whose it is to judge of the true sense and interpretation of the Holy Scriptures, hath held and doth hold; or even contrary to the unanimous consent of the Fathers."

This norm, set forth so succinctly by the Council, enables us to lay down two principles, to which all theologians subscribe:

*First:* That the principal intention of God in revealing to us the truths of Religion was to teach us all that is necessary or helpful in matters pertaining to Faith and Morals for the upbuilding of Christian Doctrine. Hence Divine Providence will always protect the Scriptures and their substantial integrity will always be preserved; and proper guides and interpreters will never be wanting (the Church and the Fathers). Usually it is not difficult to discern what "pertains to Faith and Morals." It may happen, however, that certain factors play a very important part in the plan of Divine Providence, and for this reason may fall under the heading of "Matters of Faith." This is verified in those instances wherein the fact or quality is conformable or suitable to the end intended by God. For this reason it is considered as redounding to the beauty and perfection of revealed Religion, and to that extent constitutes an object of Faith directly revealed. On these grounds many are of the opinion that the *"modus formationis"* of the body of the first man pertains to the content of revelation directly intended by God.

*Secondly:* All other truths are revealed concomitantly, or, as many say, *"Per accidens"* as was explained above. Apropos of these we need only remark that (1) in these descriptions or assertions, the inspired authors did not fall into any error; (2) that great latitude is permitted exegetes; (3) when it is certain that the facts or circumstances were written by the human Authors in consequence of certain knowledge, with the intention of stating them as objectively true, in a certain definite sense, they must be accepted as such. If the sense is ambiguous, no exegete or theologian may insist upon the acceptance of one interpretation in preference to the opposite one. But the Church may, if circumstances or necessity warrant such a course, pronounce definitively upon the point in question. Many modern scholars are of the opinion that the descriptions of the formation of Adam as contained in the sacred Document are not so clear as to exclude all reasonable doubt concerning the intent of the Author. For this reason they hold to the view that the formation of the body of Adam as explained by the more moderate Evolutionists is just as compatible with the literal truth of Scripture as is that proposed by their more rigorous opponents.

Now the question quite logically presents itself: Has the Church uttered any definition on this point, or has she by her actions condemned the more modern opinion?

Since the Church alone speaks for herself, it will be necessary to consult the ecclesiastical documents wherein reference is made to this highly controversial topic.

Before proceeding further, however, it will be well to consider the various vehicles through which the Church makes known her mind in matters pertaining to Faith and Morals. To find out what the Church teaches on any question, we must consult the declaration of the Church herself, and if there be nothing to indicate that she has spoken clearly upon any matter, we are not justified in foisting our views upon those who differ with us. In this respect it is well to remember the directive and effective norm given us by the Church in this connection; in Canon 1323 we read: "Nothing is to be taken as dogmatically declared or defined unless it is manifestly known to be such." The usual sources to which we must go, in order to learn whether a given doctrine conforms to or is at variance with the teaching of the Church, are:

1.  The Solemn Magisterium of the Church, as manifested in her
    (a) Pontifical Definitions "Ex cathedra";
    (b) Definitions formulated by Ecumenical Councils;
    (c) Symbols and Professions of Faith held by the Church Universal;
    (d) Definitions of Particular Councils when approved by the highest Authority in the Church in a solemn manner; that is, with the intention of binding all the members of the Church.
2.  The Ordinary and Universal Magisterium of the Church, as evidenced in
    (a) Doctrines obviously connected with the practices obtaining in the Universal Church . . . such as the administration of the Sacraments;
    (b) Doctrines unanimously taught by the Fathers and Theologians as divinely revealed;
    (c) Doctrines evidently contained in Sacred Scriptures.

3. In addition to the above-mentioned sources, it is necessary to include the authoritative pronouncements made by the Supreme Pontiff and the Organs employed by him in dispatching the work of the Church; usually these organs are referred to as Congregations.

In order to expedite the solution of this problem, it will suffice to consider the tenets of evolution in accordance with their compatability with the teachings of the Church as outlined under the three headings given above.

With regard to the first, that is, the Solemn Magisterium of the Church, we can safely state that the matter has not been defined. The only *"ratio dubitandi"* is found in the decree of the Council of Cologne and its relation to the fourth statement made under this heading. The Particular Council of which we speak was held in the year 1860. It stated: "Our first parents were immediately created by God." "Hence we declare openly opposed to Holy Scripture and to the Faith the opinion of those who go so far as to say that Man, as far as his body is concerned, was produced by the spontaneous transformation of the less perfect into the more perfect, successively, ultimately ending in the human."

Recalling what was stated above that a Particular Council's Decrees are definitive and of a dogmatic character only when they are solemnly approved by the Supreme Authority in the Universal Church, and realizing that such an act of endorsement is not in evidence, we are constrained to admit that this decree has no binding effect on the Church at large. Perhaps it was the intention of the Council to condemn the opinion that maintained the evolution of the human body as purely *spontaneous* up to and including its ultimate term; that is, the individual human nature as such. This opinion is absolutely untenable, for such a theory excludes God from the process, and there is no doubt that the Council was unwilling to admit such an explanation of the origin of Man. Christian Naturalists posulate the intervention of God, and ascribe the perfection of the work to the hand of God; but, regardless of the intent of the Council, the fact still remains that there is no record of its having received that formal and solemn approval of the Supreme Pontiff that is required for a dogmatic definition.

II. Has the Church, in her Ordinary Magisterium, ever condemned the doctrine of Evolution in its modified form? Acting in accordance with the principle already laid down, and expressed in the Code of Canon Law, it seems that a negative answer must be rendered. Certainly it is difficult to understand how the Holy See, *Custos integerrima Fidei,* could tolerate the spread of this teaching which is held by so many Catholics, and remain indifferent, if the theory were evidently opposed to Revelation and the teaching of the Church. It is a fact that the more rigid view was universally held until a short time ago, and we know that quite a few theologians considered the universal acceptance of what seemed the obvious meaning of Sacred Scripture to be an indication of the true doctrine held by the *Ecclesia Discens;* but we must realize that the Church through her Supreme Authority has the sole right to pass judgment upon the dogmatic value of a conviction that has gained universal favor among the people and scholars. As was stated above, the sense of Sacred Scripture is preserved whether we accept or reject Evolution, and the Church had no reason for correcting or sustaining those who, in the absence of formal definitions or declarations, held views that seemed to accord with the findings of the sciences, or, at least, were not opposed to the same. If we recall the notions that prevailed, until a short time ago, regarding the universality of the Flood, which opinion resulted from an interpretation (erroneous, perhaps) of the inspired Text, we shall see how careful we should be before asserting that any *apparent* meaning of Holy Writ that has to do with the sciences is the *real* meaning.

Since, therefore, the Ordinary Magisterium of the Church, as a norm for judging the infallible truth of a revealed doctrine, must include the endorsement or acceptance on the part of the Church itself, considered officially, and since we have no evidence that such ratification has taken place, it seems that we are justified in asserting that the doctrine of Evolution has never been condemned, for the simple reason that the contrary has not been proposed as the sense of Divine Revelation in such a manner as to exclude all doubt in this connection.

III.  With regard to the third category mentioned above: non-infallible teachings, especially as propounded by the Congregations—there is greater difficulty experienced in reconciling the stand of the Evolutionists with the pronouncements issuing from High Authority.

We may not lose sight of the fact that the Congregations are employed by the Supreme Pontiff as aids in managing the affairs of the Universal Church.  At times the Pope may give his endorsement to certain Decrees of these Congregations so to make them his very own, thereby exercising the office of Universal Teacher. But usually when he approves the Acts of the Congregations he does it in such a way that the Acts are really those of the respective Congregation.  However, to such Decrees of the Roman Congregations, religious and prudent assent must be given, and this assent must be internal, not merely apparent.  This is true especially of the Decrees of the Biblical Commission, as stated by Pope Pius X.  To the Decrees of this Commission we shall now turn our attention.

On June 30, 1909, the Biblical Commission declared that "we may not call in doubt the literal historical sense of Genesis with regard to the special creation of Man (*peculiaris creatio hominis*)" . . . which undoubtedly means that man was the object of a special creation.  Now does this involve the rejection of the evolutionary hypothesis regarding the origin of man's body by organic evolution?  To many such seems to be the case.  But a careful analysis of the Decree has led many others to the opposite conclusion.  If exactness is to be sought anywhere it is certainly in decrees of this nature.  Obscurity must always militate against the legislator.  Surely no one is bound to admit that Adam's body (the object of discussion) was *created* in the proper sense of the term. In our rigid interpretation of Genesis we are accustomed to refer to it as having been "formed" from the earth.  The only part of man that is immediately created is the spiritual soul.  Exponents of the new opinion call attention to the fact that the Decree does not specify the "first man"; whence these Authors deduce that the decision (*peculiaris creatio*) applies not only to Adam but to all men.  Bishop Laminne, of Liege, former teacher of Dogmatic Theology in Louvain, makes the following statement anent this: "In the Decree of the said Commission there is nothing against the general doctrine of Evolution, or against the opinion which attributes to evolution the formation of the body of the first man. Indeed, it is affirmed, not without grave authority, that the words of the reply of the Biblical Commission concerning the first chapters of Genesis were chosen in such a manner that this opinion should not be excluded."  The grave authority here referred to is, by common report, the one who was then Secretary of the Biblical Commission, Dom Laurent Janssens, a theologian of first rank.

In addition to the above we must consider the cases of Fathers LeRoy and Zahm.  Both of these scholars, in accordance with the trend of the times, proposed a modified form of Transformism. The principal fault in LeRoy's teaching seems to have been his denial of *any* special intervention on the part of God in the formation of Adam's body, other than the creation and infusion of the spiritual soul.  Zahm contended that, while some Catholics postulated a special divine intervention, for the formation of Adam's body from a lower organism (animal), he did not agree with them.  In due time these authors were invited to Rome to render an accounting.  LeRoy answered the summons, but Zahm was unable to do so.  The effect, however, was the same in each case.  LeRoy's book appeared in 1891 and he retracted in 1897. In 1899 Father Zahm withdrew from circulation the work he had published two years previously.  As the result of these developments, the question regarding the "descent" of man from a lower animal seemed to many to have been definitely settled in the negative.

But what explanation may we give for the "about-face" of many present day writers?  How can we reconcile the present attitude of the Roman Congregations with the stand presumably taken two-score years ago?  That there appears to be a certain degree of forbearance, which was not in evidence then, cannot be denied. Certainly many present day commentators take a broader view than we find in representative writers of the early part of the present century. Almost invariably the latter contended that the claims of the Transformists, in so far as they affected the descent of man, were altogether untenable. They did not go so far, except in a few cases, as to brand this form of evolution heretical, but the leading authors maintained that it was a dangerous doctrine, entirely irreconcilable with the teachings of the Fathers, and, by implication, with the revealed doctrine contained in the Scriptures. Usually these authors were prudent enough to refrain from branding it with any kind of "theological note." But now the pendulum is beginning to swing in the opposite direction.

Father Cuthbert Lattey, S.J., former Professor of Sacred Scripture at Saint Beuno's and now Professor of Theology at Heythrop, who wrote the preface to one of the latest works on this topic, Dr. Messenger's *Evolution and Theology,* approves the Author's accepting the general principles of Evolution for the purpose to be achieved by the book; that is, the clearing up of the theological issue, and he does not hesitate to express the opinion that Father Messenger is "safe." He declares, further, that the Holy See does not seem minded to give an authoritative pronouncement on the point; and he expresses himself to the effect that the signs do not lead us to expect any decisions of the Holy See upon this question.

Rev. Father Souvay, D.D., S.S.D., President of Kenrick Seminary, also praises Dr. Messenger for his efforts in clearing up a difficult question between Science and Theology.

Surely this is entirely different from the position maintained by the Catholic Scholars of a generation ago, when theories were proposed far more moderate than some propounded at the present time. There still lingers the recollection of the violent attacks that were made upon Mivart by the philosophers, theologians and many scientists of his day. Although his work was never officially branded, and although he was signally honored by Pope Pius IX, nevertheless his teachings were considered too radical and too closely akin to those of Darwin to meet with acceptance.

The limits of this paper will not allow me to take up in detail the cases of LeRoy and Zahm. Father LeRoy tells us that he withdrew his book because, after examination by competent authority, it was found untenable. In this connection, Dr. Messenger, who made a careful study of all the evidence obtainable, vouchsafes the opinion or suggestion that the "competent authority issuing the order" was none other than Dr. LeRoy's Religious Superior, the Father General. But, admitting that the Decree emanated from the Holy Office or the Index, it does not necessarily follow that because it was forbidden to LeRoy and Zahm to teach such doctrines that these were thereby declared to be absolutely false and contrary to the Faith. To the unbiased observer it indicates extreme prudence, wisdom and watchfulness. But at a later date, in 1909, when official pronouncement was made by the Biblical Commission regarding matters connected with the point in question, the terms used, as we have seen, were not such as to imply that the question must be taken to be a closed one.

For the reasons contained in the foregoing pages, I believe Catholic scholars are permitted freedom of opinion in this matter and that discussions on the point at issue are allowable, unless and until the rightful Authority speaks clearly.

# SOME PROBLEMS OF ADMINISTRATION IN OUR CATHOLIC HIGH SCHOOLS

THERE have always been some problems of administration in our high schools and it may be sincerely hoped that there always will be, for problems are indigenous to progress. As a matter of fact, progress only derives from the apprehension and solution of new problems as they arise.

Mr. Chesterton has facetiously remarked that we Americans love problems but are not so keen about solutions. I should like to accept that statement as a keen observation, and immediately add that it seems to me to be true not only in fact but also in principle. In a democracy we must make some allowance for the freedom of others. We must come to a solution of problems, not only theoretically, but also practically. It is not enough that the solution of a problem be apprehended by "the best minds"; it must permeate down to the masses, and finally be adopted or rejected by the ballot.

For this reason, discussion of problems does form an integral part of their solution. It may be a tedious, inefficient and provokingly long-winded way to solve them; but that is part of the price of democracy. And it is precisely in this spirit of discussion that this paper is offered for your perusal and digestion.

Fundamentally, of course, all our problems boil down to the one all-important question, "What do we wish our high schools to do?" That widespread dissatisfaction is voiced with the whole school system of the United States, is patent. It is everywhere said that our educational system has not succeeded as it should. But it is all very easy to indict the whole system; it is not quite so easy to indict the causes. And yet, unless we correctly diagnose the affliction, we labor in vain to effect the cure.

May it not be that the causes are so all-pervading that they escape the casual eye? I am of the opinion that this is so.

The educational system of the United States has risen and grown to its present stature through years of bewildering changes in our whole national life. Let anyone above the age of forty look back and try to list the changes that have transpired and the trends that have risen and fallen in that comparatively short space of two score years. To list any one of them and show its ramifications in the life of the people would take us far beyond the scope of this paper. The important point, not to be overlooked, is that fundamental changes have occurred in our family and social life. Particularly, we are becoming more social minded. We think in larger units. The State is slowly superseding the Family. Little by little, it is assuming more and more of the obligations of the parents. We may not agree that this is a good thing. We may be actually fighting this trend. But the important point is not to overlook or ignore it.

Nor can we blithely assume that this is being done over the protests of our Catholic people. Caught in the vortex of complex economic and social whirlpools, parents are being whisked along with the current whether they wish it or not. My own personal opinion is that they are not struggling overly hard against it. Human nature is fundamentally lazy. Sloth is still one of the capital sins. And it is very comforting to have the children taken off our hands a few years earlier and kept under surveillance a few years longer. It is nice to know that Johnny or Jane will be under competent guides, who are vigilant to detect and anxious to probe the slightest defect, physical or mental.

Furthermore, many parents approach the subject with a definite inferiority complex. To them this is all bewildering; and it is done in the name of progress. They dare not resist what they do not comprehend. It may well be assumed here that parents definitely are not against the present educational trend in this country. Perhaps in some isolated cases, yes! but in the vast majority of cases, no.

Now, the problem that confronts our Catholic high school in the United States derives from the changing attitude on the part of parents as well as the assumption of more duties on the part of the state. What are we to do about it? Again the question is, "What do we expect our high schools to do?"

Almost any day one can pick up some Catholic periodical and

find there a lament on the passing of the classical subjects from our schools. Not that the classical course is definitely abandoned, but that the lessening number of applicants for these subjects bodes ill for the future. Now, the classical course is an integral part of any high school curriculum, and as such it ought to be encouraged and, at times, even insisted upon. But it seems to me that the main problem that faces us here is, not how many students we can get to enter the classical course, but how many other courses we can get into the curriculum for the convenience of the pupil.

Among the important changes that have transpired, a fundamental place is held by the broadening base of education. Children are being kept in school for longer periods. Economic and social changes have sent many more children to our high schools than was the case in former years. There was a time when the Catholic high school could pride itself on a solid classical course, preparing men for advancement to higher studies in the colleges. But that day is past. Today the greater proportion of our students will not enter college, and has no intention of preparing for it. Even of those who propose to go on, many will select technical schools and not the arts course. And so, on the whole, we can well assume that the majority of those who enter our high schools do not desire the traditional course but more practical subjects.

Now, laboratories are expensive enough, but shops for these practical arts are positively prohibitive. Here is a grave problem of administration. Faced with it, many a principal is forced to see students enter the public schools. A Catholic manual training school would be a real boon, but we are far from that desired goal in almost every diocese. A city in the State of New York faced a similar problem realistically, when forced to curtail expenses; and, to a great extent, it succeeded in solving the problem. The school system arranged with local artisans—plumbers, electricians, tailors, etc.—to allow students to spend an hour or two daily under supervision either in the shops or on the job. Regular attendance was required just as for the usual class period, and regular credits were granted for the work done. Thus school shop work was superseded by supervised shop work on actual projects, and very good results were obtained.

Ours is a vast country. No one solution will be found acceptable everywhere in it. But this problem of accommodating ourselves to the pupil, instead of insisting that he accommodate himself to our curriculum, is of real importance and needs some solution to be found for it. It is to be feared that many administrators merely overlook it. Many diocesan institutions hold competitive examinations for admission, and thereby practically eliminate a large group who actually are more in need of Catholic guidance.

Of course, many a principal or supervisor will say that this is a matter of higher authority. Without doubt, their claim can be allowed. But is it not true that they personally could do more by earnest endeavor to solve the problem—by acknowledging its existence, by calling it for discussion at meetings, by discussing the advisability of outside arrangements? It seems to me that this finally simmers down to a realization of the fact that we are dealing individually with human beings—SOULS.

This I consider the second (if it be not really a continuation of the first) great problem of administration, that is, to individualize our pupils, to cease grouping them in our mind as a school or a class, and to see them somewhat as Christ saw men of His time, not as a herd or a crowd or a rabble, but as individual souls. To develop this point of view in himself and in his teachers will tax the skill and ingenuity of any principal.

It might be objected that this is primarily a problem of class procedure and not of administrative jurisdiction. But the objection betrays an attitude that should be corrected. From the administrative point of view, the child should be considered as an individual: he should not be thrown lightly into classes that happen to suit the convenience of the principal or the prefect of studies. It is again a case of fitting the curriculum to the pupil, not vice versa. It is a difficult problem because it involves additional work and coöperation on the part of an already overworked teaching staff. The principal cannot hope to be able to interview and allocate all the incoming students; and for this reason he must enlist the assistance of the teachers. As a matter of fact, I feel strongly that to our teachers should be assigned a greater share in the administrative duties of the principal or supervisor. With their staff curtailed to a minimum, these latter cannot hope to attend to all the actual work that is desirable.

Teachers could be enlisted in the rôle of Student Guides; and, if they carried on their work conscientiously, the efficiency of the school would soon increase by a hundred per cent. It is the fundamental problem of viewing the pupils as individual human SOULS. Seen in this light, guidance becomes not merely an added burden but a participation in the Apostleship of Christ. To interview the pupil, to strive to fathom his strengths and his weaknesses, to encourage, to exhort, to direct; in short, to make of our high school a real ALMA MATER—this is not a new job —this is Apostleship. How many problems in discipline, in study, in emotional life might not be forestalled or lessened by such coöperation on the part of the faculty. Difficult, yes. Time consuming, yes. But if, within the hearts of our Catholic teachers, the zeal of Apostleship glows more ardent than the fire of peda-gogy, then guidance will be a labor of love, helpfulness will be a source of delight, and religion will vitalize the curriculum. Religion must be the basis of ultimate success in a Catholic high school.

This leads us to a third very pressing problem of administra-tion in our high schools—the better integration of Religion with the curriculum. Much has been said and written upon this subject, upon the failure of the class in Catechism, upon the lack of spirituality in many of our graduates, upon the lack of Catholic leadership in them, and the like. Much, too, already has been done to correct this. Many excellent courses in Chris-tian Doctrine have made their appearance during the last few years. Sodalities have been instituted. Catholic Action is now being intensively stressed. Yet, in many of our high schools, much remains to be effected in these respects.

The urgent need of the Church today is an informed laity, a goodly portion of Catholic lay writers and leaders of thought. Accepting that most of those who enter our high schools will not get the advantages of a Catholic college education, it devolves with increasing urgency upon the secondary schools to intensify their training along religious lines. We must send forth graduates skilled, not only in the humanities, but in the knowledge and the service of God. It would be utter folly to measure the success of a Catholic high school by the amount of religious knowledge it imparts to its pupils. That knowledge must be so imparted and exemplified that it will lead its recipients to love and service, love of God, love for the Church, and willing service—in a word, Catholic Action. If the Catholic high school fails in this, it does not attain its purpose. We might well accept as the criterion of success, not the records of accrediting agencies, but the records of the Catholic lives and achievements of our graduates.

But this intensifying of religious training and closer coördination of it with the other classroom subjects requires much thought and planning, if it is to attain the degree of success it deserves. And here again the coöperation of the faculty is a prerequisite. In fact, any extra work assumed by the high school principal in our Catholic high schools is so dependent upon extra work by the faculty also, that the question of teacher coöperation becomes a problem in itself. Teachers, I feel sure, will willingly coöperate when they see the administrative point of view. But they are human beings; they will not take upon themselves new burdens nor seek new means of increasing their spheres of influence in the school, unless they feel certain that the school superiors are sympathetic to new ideas.

In this matter of enlisting teacher coöperation I strongly favor regular faculty seminars where principal and teachers all meet upon the common level of teachers discussing their problems. This equality is essential if the principal is to avoid the impression of merely dictating commands. It might be well even to elect a chairman for each meeting in order to engender a feeling of freedom and equality. At the first session, discussion might center around our first problem stated above, "What do we expect our high school to do?" It should be agreed upon readily that, first of all, the school must come up to the requirements of the accrediting boards, or it shall cease to be a recognized school. The need of a good course of studies, of a library, of laboratories will then probably be discussed from the point of view of scholastic standing.

Here may be introduced the idea that these things are all desirable and indeed necessary; but, since our schools are Catholic schools, we need to take a different viewpoint of scholastic matters. Our task is not only to prepare youths for the happy life here in human society; our duty is preëminently to educate them for a fuller participation in the life of Grace. This is the introduction to the idea of the Apostleship of Teaching. An outline of the work that should be accomplished by a Catholic high school is then in order.

The approach to the pupil as an individual can be insinuated easily in the light of the dignity of the human soul. The teacher can more readily see the task in the light of the ultimate objectives of education, instead of as a purveyor of facts of knowledge. I think it will be a peculiar teacher in a Catholic high school who can reject participation in the work of administration, when placed upon this basis.

In using the phrase, "participation in the work of administration," I mean exactly that. The coöperation of the teaching staff in this matter of religious training and guidance should be considered as a part of the administrative work assigned to individual members of the faculty. In this capacity they should be left pretty much to their own devices and initiative. Of course, minimum norms of procedure are inevitable, but, beyond these, the less interference the better. Teachers should be backed to the limit by higher authority. And discrepancies in technique or good judgment can be ironed out at the faculty seminars, where the combined moral force of the entire faculty should serve as a corrective to hare-brained proposals or procedure.

Great stress has been laid on this idea of faculty seminar because, in my opinion, it is very important in our Catholic schools to enlist the enthusiastic support of the teachers. Our administrative offices are so badly understaffed, as a rule, that it is imperative to enlist teacher coöperation, if we expect to broaden our field of usefulness to the Catholic pupil. On the other hand, our teachers are usually Religious or Priests. In one case, they may act solely through obedience and lack the initiative necessary for the successful coöperation in administrative work. In the other, too great a share of initiative may be encountered to the detriment of the plan as a whole. The faculty seminar, properly handled, should serve in the first case as the efficient magneto; in the second, as a vigilant governor.

With faculty coöperation, the principal and supervisor will find added courage to face changing problems as they arise, to bring them to the attention of the teachers, and to seek further assistance in pushing forward the outposts of Catholic educational service. Naturally, this will not end all problems. Many an administrative office is closed to new suggestions, darkened against the entrance of the light of new problems by almost insurmountable preoccupation with the very necessaries of scholastic existence—interest payments, amortization of debts, proper library and laboratory facilities, and a sufficient staff of teachers to handle the bare minimum of curriculum requirements.

To such, the additional burden of classes necessary to take care of the more practical courses is out of the question. Face to face with an already overburdened faculty, he will hesitate to bring up the question of giving individual attention and guidance to the pupils. The course in Religion will almost inevitably suffer for the same reason. And yet, it seems that even here the faculty seminar would be able to accomplish much that has been unsuspected hitherto. It costs little but added effort to individualize the teaching process; tutoring is not required, but more individual attention to the needs and the reasons for the shortcomings of backward pupils will not be very difficult. The eyes or the ears, the heart or the lungs may explain many difficulties and apparent dullness. Sympathetic guidance may counteract sinister home conditions. Surely these are desirable goals for any Catholic teacher.

Certainly, Religion should receive intensive cultivation in all our Catholic schools. It is the very *raison d'être*. Not only should the actual study of Christian Doctrine be highly developed, but personal piety should be inculcated. Sodalities are desirable. Regular attendance at Mass and the Sacraments should be encouraged; opportunity should be offered for attendance. Catholic Action of some sort should be entered into. In short, the whole atmosphere of the Catholic schools should be one of devotional Catholicism.

It will repay the principals of our Catholic high schools to spend some time in serious consideration of these particular problems. Other preoccupations may seem to be of greater importance, but only let us ask ourselves in all fairness, "For what purpose does this Catholic high school exist?" All other things must be subsidiary to the *Catholic* education of the pupils. It is then preposterous to expend our energies in the physical equipment of the school, and to leave undone the one task necessary. The principal and supervisor must first convince themselves that the school exists for the pupil, not the pupil for the school; that Religion is of greatest importance in our Catholic schools and therefore needs special consideration and closer integration with the whole discipline of the school. Then they must strive to educate and stimulate the teachers along the same lines.

The solutions of these few problems—if solution ever be reached—will not be a panacea for all the worries inherent in the job of administration. Problems will continually be with us; at least, it is to be hoped that they will. For when the Catholic high school principal finds he has no problems facing him, it is probably time to face the problem of finding his successor.

# SCIENCE AT THE HIGH SCHOOL LEVEL

At the present time the expression "high-school science" in its generally accepted meaning, includes the biological and physical sciences, whether they be offered as survey courses, such as General Science, or as courses in specific subjects, such as Chemistry.

The object of the present paper is to offer what may be considered a desirable curriculum in science at the high-school level and to discuss ways and means of improving science instruction in our Catholic high schools.

At the outset it will be well to keep in mind the following facts:

1. That most of the high schools in the large cities under diocesan jurisdiction, or under the jurisdiction of the teaching Orders, are regular four-year high schools for boys only or for girls only, with an average enrollment of one hundred to two hundred (few exceeding four hundred). In the smaller communities both boys and girls attend the same high school.

2. That nearly all of these schools are day schools with a scholastic year of thirty-six to thirty-eight weeks.

3. That pupils for the most part come from parochial schools with little or no previous training in science.

4. That the schools are located in widely different parts of the country and are governed by different accrediting agencies and educational associations.

5. That for the greater number of boys or girls attending our high schools, high school is a finishing school; for the smaller number, say twenty per cent, it is college preparatory.

6. That some of the schools are exclusively devoted to the training of the youth for membership in a religious order (or for the priesthood) and some are called "select"; and that, for purposes of science instruction, there should be no great difference between the science courses offered

in these schools and the science taught in the other schools (except, perhaps, that science courses offered in these should be more on the style of college preparatory).

It is also worthy of note that, in so far as science is concerned, the urgent need in the high schools is that of teacher preparation. It seems there already exist a fairly well organized science curriculum and standard laboratory equipment in most of the schools. General Science is being taught in first year; one of the biological sciences, in second year; Physics and Chemistry, in third and fourth years; and, quite recently, most of the schools have installed science laboratories that are at least moderately well equipped.

Next to the need of properly trained science instructors one may place that of a science library. Accrediting agencies are insisting upon the necessity of an adequate science library as a most essential aid in science instruction.

In the way of supplying these two present existing needs it is proposed, after the discussion of the science curriculum, to offer a plan for the training of the high school science teacher and to recommend lists of selected science books that should be on the shelves of the high school library. As a fourth topic, if space permits, "other aids" for the improvement of science instruction may be discussed.

## Science Curriculum

In recent years many very excellent studies in the reorganization of the high-school science curriculum have been made. In the eastern section of the country the New York State Regents are recognized as having attained a rather high standard. In the mid-western section the North Central Association took up the work of high-school curriculum reorganization and published the results in book form in 1933.[1] Four years ago the National Society for the Study of Education published a program for teaching science both at the high-school level and in the elementary grades.[2] An outstanding contribution on science instruction by

W. L. Beauchamp may be found in the monograph written under the direction of the Office of Education in Washington, D. C., which undertook within the last few years to make a national survey of secondary education.[3]  Many of the state universities have made special studies in the way of science curriculum-making.  Collectively these studies represent the earnest efforts of specialists well trained and experienced in curriculum-making and in the fields of special sciences.  They represent the expenditure of thousands of dollars required by investigations, clerical work, and other expenses attendant upon such activities.

One may not always adopt the same philosophy of education that is proposed by these educators, nor be governed at all times by the same general goals and specific objectives recommended by them.  But, in the main, these contributions, in addition to indicating the trends in high school science instruction, are very helpful guide posts in formulating the units of the science courses in our secondary schools.

In offering a sequence in science subjects suitable for high school students it is desirable that the courses should be designed to acquaint the pupils in an elementary way with the more important forces and laws of nature.  Furthermore, the science curriculum should be so constructed as to give pupils an understanding and appreciation of these laws and forces as they influence every-day life.  To quote from Downing,[4] "science as a part of a general education should be so taught that it will enable the average individual to apply it to the solution of those problems involving science which will arise in his life—not only those problems which demand solution because he must do something about them, but also those he attempts to solve merely to satisfy his intellectual curiosity.  This average individual needs what may be designated *consumer science* as distinct from *producer science* the science of the specialist or the research student."  Our problem then in the teaching of high school science is not so much that of training boys and girls to become scientists, as it is that of helping them to become intelligent laymen.  Emphasis should be placed upon the understanding of principles rather than upon the accumulation of details and facts. One is lost in the maze of factual material presented in textbooks of science; and, *unless the generalizations of science are stressed,* one cannot hope to obtain the mastery of those principles which form the basis for the interpretation of biological and physical phenomena. In all courses, systematic methods should be emphasized and scientific attitudes should be developed; [5] and pupils should be trained in drawing proper conclusions from established facts and principles.

At the present time the most widespread plan of offering science at the high school level is to provide a course for each year, calling the courses, if you will, Science I, II, III, and IV. It is the aim to plan these courses in such manner that there will be dependent continuity throughout the four grades and there will be no useless repetition of units that have been previously mastered. Science I and II should be required of all pupils; Science III and IV may be made elective. On the assumption that the first two courses carry with them full units of credit, the requirement of the educational associations (that each prospective graduate present two units in science) is fulfilled. Moreover, as was previously mentioned, high school for 80 per cent of the pupils that go there is a finishing school, and many (say 30 per cent) are compelled to withdraw at the end of the second year. It is certainly very desirable that these boys and girls should be acquainted with the common materials and facts in nature and should be given an understanding of these materials and facts as they influence human life. Materials out of which the earth is made; facts of the universe in general; the motion of the planets; the earth in its relationship to other bodies of the universe; the life, both plant and animal, that exists on the earth; food required to sustain life, both plant and animal; man's relation to the other beings on the earth; problems of hygiene, of clothing, of communication and of transportation—these may well be put in courses, Science I and II (more frequently called General Science and General Biology) offered in the first two years of high school. In the selection of textbooks for these courses the author has found it best to use those that treat of the fundamentals of natural science as an integrated two-year science program organized in terms of *units of understanding*.

In any course in science not more than eight or nine units should be taken up in the period of thirty-six weeks—a normal school year. There is included in this paper an outline of the course in terms of units; but, in general, it is recommended that it be left to the judgment and experience of the teacher just what units are calculated to lay the basis for the solution of the problems pupils in high schools in the different sections of the country must solve. The teacher will be guided by the vocations and avocations of the people in the particular section; by the knowledge necessary to read intelligently articles that appear in current periodicals and newspapers; by the interests displayed by pupils in the natural science fields. Nevertheless, whatever the calling in life or the particular interests of the pupils, the science offered in the first two years of high school should impart the principles by which the pupil may be enabled to solve problems of every-day life that are more or less common to all of us.

It is suggested that Science III and IV be elective and that, in accordance with general practice, they be Physics and Chemistry, respectively; or, as an alternative, that a course be offered in *fundamentals of physical science* and that such a course offer units on the nature of matter, the concept of energy, heat and temperature, transformations of matter, electricity, etc. In schools that have an enrollment of not more than two hundred such a course (fundamentals of physical science) is recommended for third- and fourth-year students combined. Or it may be better to offer one year a course in physics to third- and fourth-year students combined, and the next year a course in chemistry to third- and fourth-year students combined. Of the two subjects physics is more desirable in high school than chemistry. It is well to note here that the same plan would obtain for girls' high schools as for boys' with the possible exception of Science III (Physics), the units of which may be offered better in the reverse order stressing more sound and light than electricity and mechanics for them. At the present time it is not customary to offer courses in the specialized fields of science more than these suggested, unless the school has an enrollment of one thousand or more.

It may be well to say a word or two about the organization and method of the courses. The science courses are organized in terms of units, each of which has as its main purpose the development in the mind of the pupil of an important concept of science or the understanding of some important principle or group of principles. Each unit is introduced to the class through a discussion that is intended to make clear the nature and extent of the material to be studied, its importance, and its connection with previous work. Then, each pupil is "put on his own," and there follows a period of study during which books in both the classroom and the general school library are consulted, demonstration and individual experiments are performed, problems are solved, excursions and field trips are made. Most important of all, during this period of exploration, through further discussions and supervised study, the individual difficulties of each pupil are given close and careful attention. On occasions of school inspection one frequently hears the criticism that the teacher lectures too much and that the process of bringing out the latent possibilities of the individual pupil is not being carried out. It seems this method of "putting each student on his own" will help considerably in overcoming the fault of "lecturing too much." When sufficient time (it will vary somewhat with the individual classes and pupils) has been given to the period of exploration, appropriate tests may be given to determine when the pupils have attained a satisfactory understanding of the material. Other activities designed to aid the pupils in organizing and expressing their newly acquired knowledge will then be in order. Special interests may be taken into account through voluntary undertakings and through the activities of a science club.[6]

All of the science courses should be so arranged as to carry full units of credit; *i. e.,* three hours of lecture (as it is ordinarily called) per week and two two-hour periods of laboratory per week for 36-38 weeks. Many of the experiments in Science I could be given very well by demonstration.

In offering these units of the various science courses it is well understood that the matter of curriculum-making should not be carried out by one person in a short time. On the contrary, such a study should be directed by the concerted efforts of a committee over a long period of time (at lease several years). With this in mind these units are suggested merely as a beginning; and it is hoped that, as the various units are taught, newer and better ideas will come to light. Time and space are not available to develop fully each of the given units—to analyze each into its four or five elements, to prepare guide sheets, outlines of presentation, and tests. To do this properly requires fifteen to twenty hours for each unit.

The author does not wish to impose on a group of teachers any single system of presenting science topics and principles in preference to others; but merely, to state that in his experience the unit of understanding (with modifications to make adjustments for existing conditions in administration, in the laboratory, in the library, and in the actual arrangement of the classrooms) has been more efficient (even in college classes) than others he has tried. The point is: some system that takes into account the individual difficulties of the pupils is better than a system that neglects this very important educational factor.

## SCIENCE I.

1. How the Earth Came to Be as It is Today—Geology and Meteorology.

2. Matter—Classification of Material Substances. Survey—very elementary in nature—of modern concepts of matter.

3. Chemical Transformations of Matter—Nature and Control of Fire. Fuel values and newer types of fuel.

4. Transformations of Matter (Physical)—Condensation and Evaporation of Water. Refrigeration.

5. Energy (Work)—Harnessing Nature to Do Man's Work. Electricity and Its Uses in Modern Life—Communication and Transportation.
6. Water Supply of Modern Cities and Homes. Sewage Disposal.
7. The Work of the Body.
8. Man and Microbes.

## SCIENCE II.

1. The Obtaining of Food Necessary for Physical Life of Plants and Animals.
2. Use of Food Necessary for Plants and Animals.
3. Growth of Plants and Animals.
4. Reproduction (Lower Phyla).
5. How Do Plants and Animals Live Together?
6. Classification of Plants and Animals. } Evolution
7. Distribution of Plants and Animals. }
8. Behavior of Living Things.
   Optional units may be given on: Heredity, Adaptation, Eugenics, Conservation of Life, Evolution.

## SCIENCE III.

1. Measurements of the Properties of Matter. This will include density, pressure, weight, etc., and introduce the metric system. The Molecular Constitution of Matter.
2. Heat and Temperature.
3. Mechanics of Fluids (Liquids and Gases).
4. Mechanics of Solids.
5. Static and Current Electricity.
6. Magnetism and Electro-magnetism.
7. Light.
8. Sound.

## SCIENCE IV.

1. The Periodic System.
2. Chemical Change and the Atomic Constitution of Matter.
3. Reaction Velocity; Reversible Reactions; Chemical Equilibrium.
4. The Theory of Solutions—Ionization.
5. Oxidation—Reduction in Terms of the Electron Theory.
6. Identification of Chemical Substances—including inorganic chemistry of the metals.

7. Carbon and Some Carbon Compounds—including some aspects of modern biological chemistry; *e. g.*, vitamins, enzymes, hormones, etc.
8. Some Commercial Applications of Chemistry—The Frasch Method; Haber Process; Birkland-Eyde Process; Fixation of Nitrogen; Deacon Process; Solvay and Le Blanc Processes; Contact and Lead Chamber Processes for Manufacture of Sulphuric Acid. Some Electrolytic Processes.

### Science Teacher

As a rule the schools and colleges that offer courses for the training of teachers of science focus the attention of the pupils upon some particular field of science, such as chemistry or biology. Teachers themselves, when asked if they are science teachers, usually reply: "I am the chemistry teacher," or "I am the biology teacher." Rarely in high school circles does one meet the teacher who can say: "I am the science teacher." Yet, particularly in the small school (the school of one hundred pupils), there is need of the teacher who is equipped to handle any one of the biological or physical sciences at the high-school level. And this is really not asking too much of one teacher.

Michigan State Normal College at Ypsilanti, Mich., recognizing the need for teachers so trained, was one of the first educational schools to offer a course for the training of high-school science teachers.[7] A suggested curriculum offered in the fall of 1933 at Ypsilanti, contained the following *minimum* requirements in science:

| Subject | Term Hrs. |
|---|---|
| General Chemistry | 8 |
| Qualitative Analysis | 4 |
| Organic Chemistry | 4 |
| Botany | 8 |
| Zoology | 8 |
| Physiology | 4 |
| Geology | 4 |
| College Physics | 12 |
| Astronomy | 4 |
| Teacher Training in Science | 4 |

Of course, other subjects go to make up the complete course for the training of the science teacher.

Many of the high schools conducted under Catholic auspices have an average enrollment of two hundred or less; and, therefore, cannot afford to have on the faculty more than one or two science teachers. Furthermore, in addition to their training in science, teachers who are members of religious orders, must receive training in subjects required by the Studium in preparation for priesthood, brotherhood, or sisterhood. In the event that science be offered in each of the four years of the high school and only one science class be necessary in each year, some thirty hours of science should be taught each week. This is more than the average load of one teacher; and, a second teacher, who could also carry most of the mathematics taught, would be required.

It is desirable that those preparing to teach science in the high schools obtain a B.S. degree. Then, after teaching for 2-3 years in high school with a B.S. degree, it would be well were they permitted to obtain at least a Master's degree in one of the special fields of science at a first-rate college or university. Perhaps the best reason for the 2-3 years of teaching experience is that present needs are to be satisfied and no time should be wasted in filling the present high school positions. Moreover, after a few years of actual teaching experience, one should grasp more readily the subject matter at hand and understand more thoroughly the methods of study.

By reason of the requirements of the Studium and of the different institutions of learning for a B.S. degree, it is a difficult matter to state definitely just what should be demanded of the student in the way of undergraduate training in the preparation for the priesthood, brotherhood, or sisterhood and for high-school science teaching. E. R. Downing has listed the requirements for teaching science in the several States, and these should not be overlooked in preparing students to teach science.[8] Then, again, it is desirable that our high-school teachers have as liberal an education as possible and, in planning a science-teacher-training course, one should overcome the tendency to favor the science subjects more than the humanities. If time were available, the solution of the problem seems to be the offering of a B.A.-B.S. course, the requirements of which can hardly be fulfilled in any less than five years (excluding summer sessions). In order that a beginning may be made, the following suggestions as to *minimum* requirements are offered.

| Subject | Semester Hrs. |
|---|---|
| Principles of Religion (including socio-religious problems and life problems) | 16 |
| English | 12– 20 |
| Latin | 12– 20 |
| German (or French) | 8– 20 |
| Philosophy and Social Sciences | 12– 15 |
| Education and Educational Psychology (including methods) | 18 |
| Botany | 4 |
| Zoology | 4 |
| Physiology | 4 |
| Bacteriology | 4 |
| General Chemistry | 8 |
| Qualitative Analysis | 4 |
| Quantitative Analysis | 4 |
| Organic Chemistry | 4 |
| College Physics | 12– 15 |
| Mathematics (including Algebra, Trigonometry, Analytic Geometry, Calculus) | 12– 20 |
| Elective (according to local requirements) | 10 |
| Total | 148–199 |

## Other Aids

In all probability the best list of representative books for the high-school science library is the one compiled under the direction of H. A. Webb and reprinted from the Peabody Journal of Education, Nashville, Tenn.

Under the heading of "other aids" for the improvement of science instruction, one should not omit to name certain current periodicals in the field of science and to indicate their usefulness.

| Journal | Usefulness |
|---|---|
| National Geographic Magazine | Of General Benefit |
| Nature Magazine | General Science and Biology |
| School Science and Mathematics | General Science and Physics |
| Journal of Chemical Education | Chemistry and Teaching Methods |
| Science Education | Teaching Methods |
| Science Counselor | Methods and General Information |

There are many devices for enriching the courses in science such as movies, slides, models, charts, exhibits, projects, essays and science clubs.[9]

It will be well to give, also, a number of important references for the teacher of high-school science. In Downing's Book [10] (pp. 39-48) are given the principles of biology, physics, and chemistry. And, for one interested in research studies relating to the teaching of science, reference to Science Education [11] will be of great assistance.

## References

[1] Webb, L. W., and others. *High School Curriculum Reorganization.* The North Central Association of Colleges and Secondary Schools, Ann Arbor, Mich. (1933).

[2] Powers, E. R. (Chairman), *A Program for Teaching Science,* Thirty-first Yearbook of the National Society for the Study of Education, Part I. Public School Publishing Company, Bloomington, Ill. (1932).

[3] Beauchamp, W. L. *Instruction in Science,* Monograph No. 22 of the National Survey of Secondary Education. Superintendent of Documents, Washington, D. C. Bulletin No. 17 (1932).

[4] Downing, E. R. *An Introduction to the Teaching of Science.* Chicago: University of Chicago Press (1934). p. 21.

[5] Curtis, F. D., *Teachers College Contributions to Education,* No. 163. New York: 1924. p. 48.

[6] Morrison, H. C. *The Practice of Teaching in the Secondary School.* Chicago: The University of Chicago Press (1931). Burton, W. H. *The Nature and Direction of Learning.* New York: Appleton-Century Co. (1929).

[7] *Science Education,* 17/202 (1933).

[8] Downing, *op. cit.,* p. 150.

[9] Woodring, M. N., and others. *Enriched Teaching of Science in the High School.* New York: Teachers College, Columbia University (1928).

[10] Downing, *op. cit.*

[11] *Science Education,* 16/55 (1931); 16/140 (1931); 16/233 (1932); 16/297 (1932); 17/138 (1933); et seq.

# AIMS AND OBJECTIVES OF THE HIGH SCHOOL COURSE IN PHYSICS

IN this paper it is not my intention to dwell on the aims and objectives of education in general, nor on those of the high school course or the science course, but only on the particular goal which the teacher of physics in the high school should make it his ambition to reach, at least in some measure. Of course, I do not mean to imply that we can divorce the aims of the course in physics from the aims of the other science courses, or non-science courses, but if we are able to justify the existence of a course in physics in the high school curriculum, then it should be possible for us to point out some specific aims which this course is designed primarily to attain, and which, at the same time are not attained, at least in a marked degree, by any other course in the curriculum.

## Preparation for College

In view of the fact that only sixteen per cent of high school pupils continue their education after they leave the high school, I believe that it is quite safe to say that preparation for college is definitely not one of the aims of the high school course in physics. This statement is made as a general one which allows of many exceptions.

In the specific case of the secondary schools conducted by the Augustinian Fathers in this country, I have figures for only three of the preparatory schools and for the one high school—Saint Thomas High School, Rockford, Illinois. Comparison of the number of graduates with the number of college entrants for the four years would seem to indicate that our preparatory schools send more than fifty per cent of their graduates to college while the one high school has sent only nineteen per cent in the last two years. (There were no records for '32 and '33.) Hence, we might be inclined to think that we should distinguish between the high school and the preparatory school when we state the aims of the various courses in the curriculum.

However true that may be for non-science courses, it seems to be the opinion of those who have investigated the matter that high school courses in science and particularly in physics are of no special benefit to the college freshman or sophomore. As a result of a survey by Foley, conducted in eight Indiana colleges, we find that for the same college course in physics the average grade of those who had had high school physics was only 4.1 per cent higher than that of those who had had no high school physics. From my own personal experience gained during nine years of teaching freshman physics at Villanova, I have gathered the general impression that high school courses in physics have not been of any particular benefit. I must admit that I have never made a special study of this point, but my impression is in agreement with the findings of those who have gone into this question seriously.

We are justified, then, I believe, in reaching this negative conclusion at the outset, *viz.*, the high school course in physics is not intended to be a preparation for a college course in the same subject. While this is a negative conclusion, it is nevertheless an important one because the implication contained in it has much to do with the matter presented in the course and the manner of its presentation.

## Major Goals of Science

The major goals to be attained by any science course are listed by Downing as the following: (a) knowledge; (b) skill in scientific thinking; (c) establishment of emotionalized standards. It is true that these are the major goals of any science course and in accordance with our preliminary statement it is not our intention to discuss these as such. However, these goals are proper to physics in a special way and it is our problem to indicate in what manner the high school physics course can be made to lead to these goals. Let us consider them in the reverse order to that in which we have named them.

## Establishment of Emotionalized Standards

We take up first the establishment of emotionalized standards. Among these may be listed in the very first place a feeling of admiration and of adoration for the Creator of the universe Who has established, with such precision and accuracy and with providence for the welfare of the works of His hands, the fundamental laws of nature that are the basis of the course in physics. There can be no doubt that the opportunities which are in the hands of the physics teacher to emphasize the omnipotence and the providence of God are innumerable. While it would be impractical for us to attempt to point out the enormous number of facts and principles which might be used for this purpose, let me cite just a single example. In discussing the fact that the maximum density of water occurs at four degrees Centigrade, and not at zero as we might expect, the physics teacher can easily bring to the attention of the students that if it were otherwise, lakes and ponds would freeze from the bottom up instead of from the top down, and as a result the fish in the ponds and lakes would all perish the first time such freezing took place. This fact can be mentioned as an example of the manner in which the laws of nature have been established by the Creator for the protection of His creatures.

A second emotionalized standard that can be readily developed by the physics teacher is that of admiration for the heroism and self-sacrifice of many scientists. The history of physics is a most fascinating subject, and in its study we discover the names of such men as Galileo, Newton, Avogadro, Kepler, Huygens, Maxwell, Faraday, Becquerel, Thompson, Röntgen, Planck, Einstein, Michaelson, Compton, Millikan, and many others who have devoted lifetimes to patient research, sometimes under the most trying circumstances, working only for the welfare of mankind and the extension of human knowledge, rather than for their own selfish ends.

The lives of many of these physicists are shining examples of the virtue of patience and the reward that comes from painstaking effort. For example, we might quote the remarkable work of Millikan in the determination of the charge of the electron. He began this work in 1906, and as a result of the most elaborate precautions for the elimination of error and for the detection of those errors that were impossible of elimination, obtained, in 1916, a result that is looked upon by all scientists as one of the most accurate determinations of a physical quantity that has ever been made. Examples such as this one, which may be brought home to the student at various points in the physics course, will serve to develop in him a respect and admiration for the work of these men and at the same time produce the conviction that the advice of experts such as these is worthy of great credence. And is not the need of advice and the necessity of listening to those who are qualified to speak, one of the most important lessons that youth needs to learn?

Another emotional standard that is very desirable in the youth of our day is respect for law. Physics, with its laws of nature that are seen to be so regular and exact and from which there is no exception, provides an excellent method of instilling respect for law and authority into the minds of the young. It is conparatively easy for the physics teacher to draw the analogy between physical and moral laws. We can point out that the consequences of our failure to observe the moral law will follow just as surely as do the effects, for example, of gravitation. But perhaps we delay too long on this particular goal of the physics course which is after all, a secondary one. Let us proceed to the second goal; skill in scientific thinking.

## Scientific Thinking

It is scarcely necessary to point out the utility of scientific thinking for the solution of any problem, be it scientific or not. Of course, by scientific thinking we mean nothing more than straight, logical, correct thinking along the lines that are peculiar to science. Perhaps it might be well to recall briefly how the scientific method proceeds and to point out the value of the method in the problems that arise in the daily lives of all of us. The teacher of science and especially of physics should not only make use of this method for the solution of his own personal problems and for the solution of problems in the classroom; but he should point out to the pupil the various steps he is taking, so that the pupil may obtain a clear insight into the method and thus acquire facility for himself. It is a pedagogical principle that we learn best by doing, and so the pupil should be trained in the scientific method by actually applying it to the solution of problems in the physics course.

The first step in the process of thinking scientifically is to gather data. This, of course, follows only after the existence of a problem has been established, and that problem has been clearly defined. He would be a poor scientist, indeed, who set out to gather data without a specific problem in mind. The gathering of data leading to a false conclusion even under the most logical reasoning is found in the teaching of Aristotle regarding the rate at which bodies fall under the influence of gravity. His inaccurate observations led him to conclude that the heavier bodies fall more rapidly than the lighter ones; hence, that the rate of fall of a body is a property of matter. If his observations, and therefore, his data had been more accurate he would have seen that the rate of fall is independent of the amount of matter a body contains. The data gathered for the solution of a problem ought to be extensive and gathered under a variety of conditions.

After the data has been collected, the next step is to analyze and synthesize what has been found. This is, perhaps, the most important and at the same time the most difficult part of the scientific method. It is necessary that we be able to select the essential elements contained in the data that has been gathered, and to eliminate all that is not essential. It is important, too, to regard unlikenesses as well as likenesses, in order to analyze our findings properly.

After we have made an analysis of the results obtained, it then becomes necessary to derive some conclusion in the form of a hypothesis or theory. Usually, the formulation of a theory comes about only after one or more hypotheses have been tried in a large number of cases. One of the tests of our hypothesis or theory, as the case may be, is the ability to predict results of further experiment. An example of the failure of a hypothesis in the prediction of results is seen in the early eighteenth century notion as to the nature of heat. At that time the caloric hypothesis was offered to explain various heat phenomena. Count Rumford reasoned that if heat is a material substance which passes from one body to another, then a body should increase in weight when it becomes heated. So he weighed a cannon that was to be bored, and the boring tool; after the boring was completed both were weighed again, and although a great amount of heat had been generated in the procedure, neither the cannon nor the boring tool had increased in weight. This fact was interpreted by Count Rumford to indicate that the caloric hypothesis was not true. On the other hand, there is the very striking and important example of Maxwell's Electromagnetic Theory of Light. Through the careful and accurate assembling and coördinating of data, Maxwell, after years of patient examination and analysis, formulated the now famous equations which bear his name. From a further consideration of these equations he concluded and predicted that it should be possible to produce electrical waves of the same nature as those of light. Hertz undertook the task of verifying this conclusion, and as a result we have today—The National Broadcasting Company.

Another very important factor in the scientific method is unprejudiced judgment. We must be willing to give assent to the facts brought before us regardless of the effect that the conclusions drawn from them may have upon us personally.

A very striking example of the effect of prejudice is found in the case of Galileo. The facts that he presented as a result of his experiments with falling bodies dropped from the Leaning Tower of Pisa showed without doubt that all bodies fall with the same speed in spite of differences in weight. But this conclusion was contrary to that of Aristotle which we have already mentioned; and hence, it was rejected because of this great prejudice in favor of Aristotle; and more than that, Galileo was expelled from the University of Pisa for daring to teach a doctrine opposed to that of Aristotle. The great Sir Isaac Newton was guilty of this same fault. He observed that water waves bend around the corners of abstacles placed in their path. This bending was not seen in the case of light, so Newton, because of prejudice, refused to accept the wave theory of light. As a result of his refusal, the prejudice of others in his favor retarded the acceptance of this theory for almost one hundred years.

Thus far we have dwelt with the inductive process in our discussion of scientific thinking. While this is most important for the formulation of hypotheses and laws, yet the other side of the method, deduction, is probably of more importance to the everyday problems that arise. Deduction is more or less the direct opposite of induction. By induction we go from specific cases to general principles; by deduction we pass from the general to the particular. Here the important point is to select the proper principles from those that we know, and to apply them to the problem at hand.

### Knowledge

Perhaps this part of the scientific method can best be considered after we have discussed the third main goal of the high school physics course, which we have called knowledge. To quote Downing:

> "Two methods of instruction are conceivable in preparing pupils to meet the problematical situations involving scientific knowledge that will arise in their lives: (1) One may list all such problems that occur in the community and make pupils skillful in meeting each, teaching them how to do each specific thing. (2) Or one may give them an understanding of the priciples of science that are most often needed to solve such problems and then may drill them in solving problems under such principles, leaving them to think through such other problems as shall occur in their later lives."

If the physics course is to be justified in the high school curriculum then we have a right to expect that it shall be of some benefit to the student after he has left the classroom. No one can doubt that the number of problems that arise in the daily lives of most people whose solution depends directly on the principles of physics, is very great. It is readily seen, then, that the first method mentioned by Downing is of no practical value. It would be impossible for the physics teacher to begin to enumerate and solve these problems. For example, one of the most common mechanisms met with in our daily lives is the automobile. In order to take care of this particular piece of machinery it is necessary to know how to do 399 different things. On the other hand, there are only twelve principles underlying these three hundred and ninety-nine operations. And the same sort of statement can be made with regard to other things. The operations are many, but the principles are few.

The logical and reasonable thing to do, then, in the high school physics course is to teach these fundamental principles and the way in which they may be applied to problems, and let the pupil learn for himself the numerous applications that will occur later. The second half of this statement is just as important as the first. It is not sufficient to instruct the student in the principles so that he can recite them from memory without fail. It is also necessary that he be drilled in the solution of many typical problems, so that he may see for himself how the principles may be applied. In other words, the deductive part of scientific reasoning is to be brought into play. Since, in the solution of problems in later life, one of the very important factors is to find the particular principles that will apply to the problem at hand, it is essential that the problems that are given in the course as typical ones on which the student may test his skill, should not be grouped according to the principles that are needed in the solution. If this mistake is made and a group of problems is given as an exercise after a principle has been learned, which problems may be solved by the application of that particular principle, then half, and the more important half of the work, is already done for the student. In this way one of the goals of the course is not attained. It is a rather common thing to find that problems are arranged in exactly this way in high school texts.

## Textbook

At this point we might consider the qualifications to be sought in a physics textbook. Of course, it is understood that one of the serious difficulties to be encountered in this matter is the fact that in many instances the State Board of Education or the particular accrediting agency under which our schools operate, and with whose regulations we must comply, specifies one or more texts to be used as standards for the various courses in the high school curriculum. If this be the case there is little or no choice left to the teacher. But if the matter is in the hands of the teacher, then he should consider, in selecting a text, that one of his goals is to teach the fundamental principles of the science and not the almost innumerable facts, which are found to clutter up so many of our modern textbooks.

In determining which principles are the most important or fundamental, we ought to consider among other things the locality in which we are placed. If, for example, the majority of the students in the school come from farms, then the teacher should lay stress on those principles which find their application in farming and the use of farm machinery. If, on the other hand, the larger portion of the student body may be expected to spend their post-school days in a factory, then a different set of principles, or at least, some different principles, will be found to be of more value.

These, then, are the goals, the aims and objectives of the high school course in physics. The teacher of physics ought to keep these aims before him as he teaches his class, so that his work may bear fruit later in the lives of his pupils. It is suggested, that since it very often happens that science courses are not popular with students, it might be helpful to point out these aims not only at the beginning of the course, but also occasionally as the course progresses. In this way the student can be brought to realize that what he is doing now will have great value in after years; thus he will feel that all his effort is not in vain.

## THE PLAN OF ORGANIZATION AND INTEGRATION OF THE GUIDANCE ACTIVITIES OF SAINT RITA HIGH SCHOOL, CHICAGO, ILLINOIS

In recent years the educational philosophy and theory which lie back of guidance in secondary education have been practically and universally accepted. Saint Rita High School has adopted the thesis that guidance of youth is one of its major functions. This program of endeavor has necessitated the inauguration of a variety of activities which will be described in this report.

The guidance of youth is a task of such complexity that it surpasses the knowledge and wisdom of one faculty member known as a guidance supervisor, working independently. The development of every desirable personal attribute which the student possesses requires that the efforts of every instructor be integrated and unified in the interest of the care and guidance of each individual pupil. Complete, positive coöperation on the part of each instructor is indispensable. In order to secure such unity and integration it is necessary to formulate plans which will provide for a thorough system of checks and balances so that information concerning a pupil may be sufficiently objective to give a basis for more accurate counsel.

The two conditions necessary for the establishment of the guidance program are: first, the interest of instructors in the pupils' problems and in becoming a power in the guidance of their students; second, having established interest on the part of the instructors, provisions must be made for the effective use of this power. Personal counseling of pupils as a specialized task becomes the particular responsibility of each faculty member. Only through the coöperation of all, may this paramount task be done in the best way.

It is in full realization of this fact that Saint Rita High School is developing its plan of guidance in such a way that they may integrate all the guidance forces within the scope of their faculty, to the end that each boy may have the combined insight of those who know him best and of those most concerned in his welfare and particularly of his moderator.

The Moderator, or Counselor, is the first agency and the basic one in the Saint Rita guidance program. The plan of organization of the school provides for the assignment of a faculty sponsor to each group of approximately thirty boys. This moderator is charged with the duty of acting as advisor to all pupils so assigned for the full four years of their high school life. The assignment of boys to these groups is made on the basis of the courses of study selected by the students. The four divisions are: the general, scientific, commercial, and the newly organized technical course. Within these large divisions the students are grouped homogeneously according to Intelligence Scores made on the Terman or Otis Intelligence Tests.

This method is advantageous in a number of ways. It gives the administration means of access to the Moderator in any situation in which a particular pupil is concerned.

A more secure bond of confidence and a direct control develops and is strengthened through the long association of student and counselor. There is an item of economy of time and energy mastered by overcoming the need of getting records of family history and case history each year. The record is accumulated during the first six months and factual information may be added constantly by the Moderator each semester. The counseling of boys demands many rather elusive items of knowledge which only continued relationship with the students and their families will disclose. The attitude of the parents toward the pupils' school aims, the economic status of the home, the general atmosphere in which the pupil lives and studies, all come through day-by-day contacts. After a moderator has had a boy in his direct charge over a period of four years there is little about the situation which he will not know if he has conscientiously endeavored to become the true confident and the ideal "Father" of the boy.

While the moderator is but one of a series of guidance agents for the student, it is through the moderator that this guidance program must operate whenever any vital question concerning the student arises.

\*　　\*　　\*　　\*

The following description of the plan of operation will present a more definite report of the procedure.

Each faculty member has two class periods each and every school week during which he meets his own guidance group for the purpose of acquainting the boys with the methods of the school, directing them in scholastic enterprise and motivating them in scholarship and character improvement.

As soon as all pupils are enrolled, the instructor begins to make an exhaustive study of the aptitudes and interest of each boy in addition to determining what factors of home environment and educational background are influencing his capabilities. The following type of record is used to summarize the results of tests, observation, and diagnosis.

### INQUIRY ON THE FACTORS WHICH INFLUENCE THE STUDY OF SAINT RITA HIGH SCHOOL BOYS

## DIAGNOSTIC RECORD

1. Name of Pupil
2. Address
3. Phone
4. Grade     1st year     2nd year     3rd year     4th year

C. A. ....................... Birth Data .................................................

M. A. ...................... I. Q. Score ...................... Test ......................

Achievement Test Score ........................... Test ...............................

A. Mental Reaction of Students.
   1. Process of Thinking.
        (a) Is the thinking accurate and fast?
        (b) Is the thinking accurate and slow?
        (c) Is the thinking inaccurate and fast?
        (d) Is the thinking inaccurate and slow?
   2. Does the student "bluff" or is he honest?

3. Does the student ask—
   (a) Intelligent questions?
   (b) Questions merely to ask questions?
   (c) Do the questions he asks pertain to the subject being discussed?
   (d) Too many questions?
   (e) Are too few questions or no questions asked?
4. Can he link up his present comprehension to his past experiences?
5. Does he have originality, inventiveness?
6. Does he depend too much on his memory to the exclusion of reasoning processes?

B. Health.
   1. Weight ................. Height .................
   2. Athletic ................. Non-athletic .................
   3. Compare him to other pupils in
      (a) Physique .................
      (b) Physical Energy .................
   4. Eyesight ................. Defect .................
   5. Hearing ................. Defect .................
   6. Teeth ................. Defect .................
   7. Speech ................. Defect .................
   8. Posture (describe).
   9. Does the pupil control his temper .................
   10. Does he show resentment on being corrected? .................
   11. Has he been seriously ill? ................. When? .................
   12. If you notice other things that should be corrected, mention them.

C. Conditions in the Home.
   1. What specific education have the parents had?
      (a) Mother ................. (b) Father .................
   2. Are both parents living?
   3. Does the student live with both parents?
   4. What language is spoken at home?
   5. Does the father work? ......... Occupation .................
   6. Does the mother work? ......... Occupation .................
   7. How many sisters does the pupil have .........
   8. How many brothers does the pupil have? .........
   9. How many sisters and brothers under school age? .........
   10. What type of home, neighborhood, and atmosphere exist? (When an instructor has a problem student, he should visit the parents' home.)

D. Student's Time Outside of School:
    1. Time of arising ............... Time of retiring ...............
    2. Does pupil eat meals at the regular time? ...............
    3. How much time is spent in duties at home?...............
       (a) Nature of duties? ...............................
       (b) Does he work for pay outside of the home? ........
       (c) Nature of this work? ...........................
       (d) How many hours are given to this work? ...........
    4. How many hours are spent in active out-of-doors exercise? ................... Inside play? ...................
    5. Does the student have a hobby? ...................
       How much time is spent with the hobby? ...................
    6. How frequently does he attend movies? ...................
       Afternoon? ........ Evening? ........ Day of the week? ...........
    7. Does he spend any nights with boy friends? ...............
       Often? ...................
    8. Is the boy a radio fan? ........ Favorite program? ...........
       Listen to radio while studying? ...................
    9. Is he fond of reading? ...................
       (a) What daily papers does he read? ...................
       (b) Sections? ...............
       (c) What magazines does he read regularly? ...........
       (d) What type of book does he read? ...............
   10. Is he a member of a club? ...............
       Frequency and day of club meetings? ...................

E. Home Study.
    1. Does student study better at home or at school? ...........
    2. Does he have a special place for study? ...............
    3. Does he have a definite time? ...............
    4. Does he follow a certain routine for studying? ...............
    5. Are the "tools" for study his own or do they belong to various members of the household? ...................
    6. What time of day does he get the best results? ...............
    7. Does he perform his own assignments? ...............
    8. How much time does he give to home study daily? ...........
    9. If he studies in the evening, is he permitted to play out-of-doors at the conclusion of his assignments? ...........
   10. Does he receive help in performing his assignments? From whom? ...................
   11. Is he frequently interrupted while studying? ...............

12. Examination Chart:

| Subjects | First Quarter | Second Quarter | Exam. | Third Quarter | Fourth Quarter | Exam. |
|---|---|---|---|---|---|---|
| 1. Relig. .... | .............. | .............. | ......... | .............. | .............. | ......... |
| 2. Latin ...... | .............. | .............. | ......... | .............. | .............. | ......... |
| 3. Gen. Sc... | .............. | .............. | ......... | .............. | .............. | ......... |
| 4. Algebra .. | .............. | .............. | ......... | .............. | .............. | ......... |
| 5. English .. | .............. | .............. | ......... | .............. | .............. | ......... |
| 6. Music .... | .............. | .............. | ......... | .............. | .............. | ......... |

13. Student remarks concerning their respective classes, instructors, etc., to their moderator:

| Date | Comment |
|---|---|
| 1. ........................... | ................................................................................. |
| 2. ........................... | ................................................................................. |
| 3. ........................... | ................................................................................. |
| 4. ........................... | ................................................................................. |
| 5. ........................... | ................................................................................. |
| 6. ........................... | ................................................................................. |

Two problems of administration which arose in regard to the Diagnostic Record were:

First, which students should be selected as the first subjects since, obviously, all could not be done at once. Second, should the counselor make the diagnosis during the bi-weekly activity period, or at a time when the presence of other students would not interfere. The advantages and disadvantages of these plans were discussed at a Faculty meeting with the resultant adoption of the following procedures:

A list shall be posted in the Faculty Room upon which each instructor is asked to inscribe the names of boys with whom they are having difficulty either due to poor scholarship or discipline. The Director or Supervisor of Studies requested each instructor to inspect this list every morning to ascertain if any pupil of his guidance group had been recorded. Diagnosis of the boy's case should be made as soon as his name appears on the list.

In the event that no member of a guidance group is listed the moderator may begin to diagnose in whatever order he wishes, either alphabetically or according to those in his judgment, who need it most.

It is recommended that instructors designate one period a week, at least, after school hours, or before school hours during which the boys are to present themselves for the purpose of diagnosis. If one or two students are interviewed each week, diagnosis of the entire group may be completed before the first semester has elapsed.

When the Diagnostic Record is completed, the results and interpretations serve as a basis for needed adjustment and, in the cases of boys who have been failing, are used for a consultation basis at the Faculty Meetings.

Insofar as time and opportunity permitted, standardized achievement tests were used to provide an objective measure of accomplishment, supplemented by school work in a given subject. In the effort to analyze the factors contributing to a pupil's achievement, both in that subject and in other subjects, examinations were made to note progress and comparative success in several subjects.

Health and physical conditions are, to a large extent, disturbing factors in the study situation. A pupil, who is not physically capable of applying himself, cannot achieve scholastic success. With this fact in mind Saint Rita High School administration provided for the examination of every student by the Oculist and Dentist. This project shall receive more adequate treatment later in the report.

Home conditions which affect study were disclosed during the interviews as being the focal point of difficulty in many instances.

The task of discovering how a pupil prepared an assignment and what methods of work he employs is indeed difficult and perplexing. The most skilled observer is not always able to discern by a pupil's physical action just what he is doing or thinking. What he does today, may not be what he will do tomorrow. Numerous hours of intimate contact with a pupil alone, such as may be spent by a moderator, will disclose many angles of a situation which otherwise would remain unknown. Many interesting case studies and their very satisfying conclusions have been reported by the moderators.

When the Diagnostic Records are completed they reveal many cases which need special care. When the personal data concerning the pupil are compiled, the pupil's scholastic success is recorded as evidenced by report card grades which are given quarterly. Thus, as soon as pupils receive their first marks from their various instructors there is available a workable profile for counseling purposes of each individual pupil.

By checking the list of Failures and probable failures posted in the faculty room, the Moderator may find one or more of his guidances group requiring special attention. A Faculty Meeting is held at which the Moderator, the Supervisor of Studies, and all other instructors are required to be present. The Moderator is requested to bring all data concerning his listed student and the student's respective teachers are requested to present his scholastic grades and endeavors.

The complaining teacher who is responsible for the listed pupil is first allowed to state his grievance, and, if he wishes, his recommendations. The other instructors are asked to contribute any pertinent information. The Moderator then, on the basis of his acquaintance with the pupil, his home conditions, and other data, makes his suggestions and recommendations. It has frequently been found that the Moderator has already diagnosed the case and is prepared to suggest the necessary readjustment at the Faculty Meeting. The objective measures of pupils are supplemented and validated by the subjective estimate of the counselor. Every case of a student in which failure or probable failure is indicated is checked by his Moderator as soon as his name has been inscribed on the Investigation List. For example, let us examine the case of Robert Schultz, who was listed as a problem case by the Latin instructor. Robert had an I. Q. of .95 and had received satisfactory grades in his other subjects, but in spite of this is failing in Latin. An examination of his scholarship record of the previous year revealed the fact that he obtained satisfactory results in his freshman Latin. On the Optical Examination Record it was recommended that Robert be provided with glasses to care for a minor defect of the right eye. This defect, however, was not considered sufficiently serious to warrant scholastic failure. It particularly did not account for failure in but one subject. It was only through the personal conference on the Diagnostic Record that the difficulty was revealed to the Moderator. The Moderator found that the method used by the second year instructor was at such variance with that of the former instructor that the boy found it impossible to adjust himself sufficiently to grasp the change. Conflicting personalities of teacher and student prevented the instructor from discovering this factor himself. Robert stated that while he did not understand what was expected, he was afraid to ask questions. Robert discussed his problem freely with his Moderator who gave a sympathetic ear and kindly advice.

The solution of the problem was arrived at by two means. First, the situation was explained to the instructor who agreed to modify his assignments to conform with the experiential background of the boy and also to provide individual attention which would bring the student to the required grade level. Second, the Moderator arranged to give the boy a half-hour private instruction weekly for the purpose of adjusting him to the method of instruction followed by his present Latin instructor. The Latin instructor reacted favorable to the Moderator's suggestion that he win the students through properly motivated lessons rather than rigid discipline. Robert is, at present, enjoying a pleasurable increasing success.

This one example illustrates definitely the ease with which perplexing problems of maladjustment have been handled in scores of cases. The active force of the Moderator, working through the Diagnostic Record method clarifies problems which may otherwise appear to be without solution.

Sympathy and understanding are the key words in all remedial and guidance work. Both may be found to be the direct outgrowth of this method of guidance.

\*     \*     \*     \*

The school which wishes to guide pupils to the development of a variety of desirable attributes must establish an adjustment of materials and methods of instruction to the capacities and needs of the individual pupil. Attention must be given to stimulation and guidance of the student's learning activities as well as to personality development. Teachers must realize that their chief function is to stimulate and guide pupil's learning, not just to impose information. Classroom activities must provide aid for more effective pupil learning.

Attention must be given to the psychology and directing of learning.

The present attitude toward learning is dynamic. Learning is considered as being an active, continuing process, which goes on after school instruction has ended. Students must be assisted in developing productive methods of independent work, so that mental activity will be continued with enjoyment and effective results. The growth of knowledge is so fast and so vast that the ability to find is of greater importance than the ability to store and recall. If the student is guided in improving his activities, and is shown that he must learn to secure knowledge on which to base this improvement, and if he is taught how to find and study knowledge, storing of facts is of lesser importance.

It is in recognition of these fundamental elements that the second function of the moderators at Saint Rita High School has been the organization and development of the Student Activity Periods. As previously stated, two periods are given over to the first and second year students to directing more adequately the study activities of these boys and to endeavoring to overcome the difficulties disclosed by the Diagnostic Record. While the difficulty of differentiating assignments to care for different ability levels within a class, motivation of assignments and other difficulties which more directly involve the teacher can be handled in Faculty Meetings, there are other difficulties which are more peculiarly the problems of the pupils.

These problems of providing the necessary tools for preparation by training in study procedures and techniques, in selection, organization and use of material and developing habits of independent work are the aims which each Moderator must endeavor to clarify for his guidance group during the Activity Periods.

The results of careful observation and tests of how high school pupils work, as reported by Symonds, Finch Charters and Messenger revealed the prime responsibility of the school in the control of time and application in study. In the entire listing of study problems reported, the need for training in specific procedures was emphasized more than any other single factor.

Using this criterion as a basis of organization the Director of Studies developed a schedule of specific topics to serve as standards of mastery in the Student Activity periods, toward the general aim of more efficient study guidance.

Consideration of study as a process leads directly to a study of learning. Study is a series of activities which are responses to situations created by an assignment. These situations have as their purpose the effecting of certain changes, such as forming habits, acquiring knowledge, awakening interests, developing appreciations, and the like. The study responses are as truly a learning activity as any response within the class period. It is the duty of the instructor to provide stimulating, interesting and worth while activities; to provide adequate facilities for obtaining desirable responses; and to guide and direct the activity of the period.

In an analysis of specific study activities required of high school students, it has been found that certain activities are common to many study situations. Activities which may be considered useful in many study situations were naturally decided upon as the basic units of the activity program. It was agreed that during the first two years the students should receive definite instruction on the following activities.

## I. Reading

In considering study procedures in which high school pupils should have systematic training, reading has been emphasized, because it is common to learning in all school subjects. By an examination of the inadequacies and weaknesses of pupils in the study process, it is found that there is frequent recurrence of inability to read effectively the material required in high school fields.

Upon the basis of the results of the Diagnostic Record the Moderator makes a diagnosis of weaknesses in the reading in order that a constructive remedial program may be planned.

Two important facts have been revealed by the scientific studies in the field of remedial reading. First, many pupils, from the first grade through junior college, are deficient in important reading skills, and second, these deficiencies can be overcome by means of intelligent and systematic remedial instruction. Many of these deficiencies are traceable to defective instruction in the early grades in the elementary school. If proper remedial instruction in the elementary school is given when needed, many cases of retardation and actual delinquency in the high school can be avoided.

While it is unquestionably true that a certain amount of individual remedial instruction will always be inevitable, the aim of Saint Rita instructors is to reduce the number of remedial cases to a minimum. This can be accomplished by an efficient program of regular classroom instruction in which the printed or written words is made use of. This program should consist of (1) rich and diversified opportunities for free reading; (2) functional reading experiences in connection with individual or group activities, and (3) systematic instruction in word recognition and the comprehension of larger units.

Every instructor must be fully cognizant of the relationship between reading ability and success in his own subject.

Definite provisions are being made for constant attention to individual pupils who encounter difficulties which they cannot overcome without special aid. The discovery of pupils who require remedial instruction is largely a matter of having instructors on the alert for individual difficulties. It has been found that teachers can usually detect the danger signals before the difficulties become dangerous.

Once the pupils in need of remedial work have been discovered, it is necessary to determine the program for improving instruction in reading.

Every supervisor or school administrator knows how practically impossible it is to revolutionize a teaching order in a short time. To achieve permanent results, it is recommended that at least one instructor attend university classes in order to become acquainted with modern reading methods, and that a definite schedule for the year's campaign be planned beforehand.

Building on the premise that limited progress is to be preferred to no advancement at all, Saint Rita High School has initiated a program of remedial reading instruction this year rather than wait for an instructor to be especially trained.

The administration agreed that responsibility for handling the remedial reading program should be vested in one instructor whose chief characteristics should be enthusiam for the work and belief in its ultimate success. Many of the remedial cases are boys who are discouraged because of past failures, and really cannot put forth their best efforts until they regain confidence. The teacher's belief in his ability to help will unconsciously communicate that attitude to them. The remedial teacher must also be systematic, patient, persistent, able to proceed in an orderly fashion, and possess a determination which does not permit the admission of failure.

The priest who agreed to undertake the program for improving reading instruction this year realized the need for being thoroughly familiar with recent research and scientific studies in the field of reading. Recent books and articles pertaining to reading, observations or accounts of current practice in teaching, and reports of previous campaigns for improving the teaching of reading and educational monographs served as source material for his guidance. Though slightly older than some of the other scientific studies the Twenty-fourth Yearbook of the National Society for the Study of Education may well be considered the best available research in the field of reading.

The students selected for special attention this year are those found to be failing in other subjects due to reading deficiencies. These boys receive remedial instruction one period a week during the Activity Period. This plan will be revised next year and at least two full periods will be allowed to the remedial instructions.

Once the pupils in need of remedial work have been discovered, it is necessary to determine the exact nature of the individual pupil's difficulty. Mere reading practice in the case of a poor reader is not sufficient. The teacher must determine the specific nature of the deficiency, locate the cause and give systematic instruction with a view to the removal of the cause.

Although very excellent results are being obtained from the current program, our new program, as it will function beginning with the new semester, will illustrate more clearly Saint Rita's Reading Guidance program.

First, some of the teachers are to be sent to the Clinical Reading classes, conducted at the University of Chicago. If they become better acquainted with modern reading methods, it will mean more intelligent coöperation from them later on.

The first step in the program for improvement will be a detailed survey of the present status of reading throughout the school. Securing accurate information is so important that this preliminary survey will be conducted in as scientific a way as possible. Among the types of information which are needed are the following:

1. Statements from each teacher concerning his own special subject, correlating the teaching of reading with his own special subject, methods used, specific problems and difficulties met with.

2. A record of available equipment including the number of books which may be used as basal and supplementary reading material.

3. A record of the extent of the pupil's reading activities, as measured by a number of pages read during the reading periods, the number of books read independently, the amount and kinds' of magazine and newspaper reading done.

4. Records of the achievement of pupils on tests of oral and silent reading, and on mental tests. Comparing the reading scores with the results of intelligence tests will show how closely pupils approach their expected achievement in reading.

These records are kept separate from the Diagnostic Record although each may prove helpful in completing the other.

After the preliminary survey has been made, the findings should be presented and discussed in group faculty conferences.

The next step is the definition of new objectives, a presentation of the aims and the making clear to each faculty man his responsibility in carrying out the program. The Instructor in Reading in conjunction with the Director of Studies shall aid the teachers in the discovery of their problems, supply specific help, and offer constructive suggestions for improving reading in all subjects.

\*     \*     \*     \*

The information gleaned from the records suggested above, with the instructor's interpretation of the data, will suggest the type of remedial service required in a given case. The material in this section will describe procedures to be used in typical cases of reading deficiency.

A.  *Motivation.*  Most cases of remedial instruction in reading are characterized by a general indifference on the part of the pupil toward reading, if not an intense dislike of reading. Boys, like adults, are fond of activities they do well, and tend to dislike those which offer great difficulty. Since the bulk of the school activities involve reading in one way or another, this general dislike often carries over to the school work in general and may result in lack of adjustment, truancy, or even delinquency. In any case, the remedial work will be immensely facilitated if care is taken to insure keen interest in the reading before remedial exercises are undertaken. Any device which will make the pupil eager to secure meaning from the printed page is useful in this connection. Of particular importance is the discovery of any special interest the pupil may have, such as a hobby, a game, a pet.

B.  *Paragraph Reading.*  Many teachers assume that a pupil who does not read well necessarily requires special drills in word recognition and they thereupon proceed to administer a dose of phonics instruction. It is true that the ability to recognize familiar words and to analyze new words is essential to good reading. Buswell found, however, that there were two major types of reading deficiency; boys who had developed the attitude of thought-getting from the printed page, but were deficient in word recognition, and boys who could recognize words but were unable to read fluently and to gather meaning from larger units. Often through overemphasis of correct oral reading or upon word recognition and phonics or through lack of abundant experience with easy, interesting material in books, boys become "word readers" and fail to develop proper habits of silent reading in the larger units. It should be recognized that the ability to derive meaning from words in thought relationships is a skill essentially different from the skill involved in word recognition.

Sometimes the difficulty may be due to a limited apperceptive background. If this proves to be true, the procedure should be to build the student's experiential background.

For the remedial program in reading there should be provided many good books and collections of poems and stories. Care should always be taken to select simple material. The purpose always is to create a habit of following the thought with a minimum attention to the individual words.

More direct and systematic instruction will frequently be needed. The commercial workbooks supply special paragraph drill. It must be observed that workbooks are not to be assigned indiscriminately to the whole class, but are to be used for remedial cases when and where needed. When scientifically prepared with a view to the development of specific skills, commercial workbooks are of great value.

C. *Sentence Comprehension.* The diagnosis may reveal that the pupil is deficient in the ability to comprehend phrases and sentences. This may be due to inadequate perception span or to ineffective habits of left-to-right movements of the eyes, or to inability to use context clues or even to lack of training in the identification of punctuation marks.

Flash card, or short exposure exercises, even at high school level, are necessary to develop a wider span of recognition and a consequent larger grasp of thought units. It has been found, however, that the mere use of flash cards carries over only in a limited degree to the normal reading situation.

Flash card drills improve the ability to read from flash cards, but do not necessarily improve reading from books. The instructor must measurably increase the amount of transfer by alternating card drills with reading exercises in books and by making clear to the pupil the purpose of the drills so that he will consciously seek to generalize the experience. The use of workbook exercises should be a part of the special instruction in these skills, just as in the case of paragraph comprehension.

D. *Word Recognition.* The ability to recognize words is essential to good reading. Such recognition depends upon a fairly large stock of sight words and upon adequate techniques of recognition of new words. If a boy is found to be without phonetic background he may be taught the traditional method of analyzing new words into the familiar sound elements and then blend these sounds into new words. The student should also have drill on associating the word with the symbol.

If difficulties in speech or in auditory acuity are in evidence, these should be removed by training wherever possible and, in any event, will serve as guidance in the type of drill necessary.

The guidance of pupils in normal reading situations involves the fundamental principle that not one but many devices should be employed in the recognition of an unfamiliar word.

E. *Speed of Reading.* In general it may be said that when specific difficulties have been overcome, speed will adjust itself. Very often undue emphasis upon speed of reading will result in a tenseness which interferes with the pupil's enjoyment of reading. On the other hand, many of the difficulties involved in reading arise from the pupil's preoccupation with individual words. In order to facilitate thought-getting the pupil should then be encouraged to read rapidly forward in order to comprehend the larger idea in the sentence or paragraph. For this purpose, a brief drill under pressure proves valuable, provided it is followed by an abundance of unsupervised reading experience with interesting material. Speed of reading, therefore, is not to be sought as an end in itself, but as a means of comprehension. Speed is to be achieved by vigorous response to individual words and by habits of reading for thought-getting through the comprehension of large units such as phrases and sentences.

Having overcome any defects in the actual mechanics of reading, the next step in the program is to outline a definite schedule of systematic training in the numerous types of reading activities which function in study. These types of reading-as-study range from uncontrolled reading for general meaning to reading as a phase of problem-solving. The types to be emphasized are: (1) rapid reading for meaning in general; (2) skimming or reading for large meaning; (3) directed or controlled comprehension, that is, the answer to definite questions; (4) outlining and summarizing material read; (5) comparing two or more presentations; (6) note-taking on materials read; (7) understanding and following directions, and (8) problem-solving. Reading is a highly complicated process. The methods used in the analysis and organization of reading procedures suggest the type of analysis which must be applied to other study activities. The determination of the specific reading procedures which function in a variety of study situations indicates the kind of techniques which must be developed for other study processes. The same scientific methods should be applied to such major activities as translating a foreign language, the learning of a vocabulary, the acquisition of fundamental processes in mathematics, the development of laboratory techniques in sciences, and the application of social and economic facts to life situations.

When a pupil has become proficient in reading ability, he is ready to receive training in other study procedures which are closely allied to reading. This brings us to a discussion of the other activities which are a part of Saint Rita Study Improvement Program.

## II. Ability to Use Books and Materials as Tools for Study

If books and other materials are to be used effectively as working tools by high school pupils, certain training must be begun early. Saint Rita's plan is not founded on a limited introduction to the use of a dictionary and possibly one ready reference book, such as an encyclopedia.

The instructor, whose duty it is to handle this division of the activity program, being fully aware of the possible aid to be had from a textbook used as a guiding tool, included it as one topical division of his outline.

There are certain principles of method to be observed in presenting this material to insure its effectiveness.

The instructor must keep in mind that a seemingly narrow skill, such as using an index or locating information involves a number of minor skills, each of which should have definite attention by teacher and pupil.

The pupils are also instructed in the use of the Glossary and Bibliography of their textbooks. This makes it possible for the student to develop the ability to seek and discover knowledge unaided.

Any real proficiency in English has as one of its elements an intimate acquaintance with the dictionary. However, students require guidance in dictionary usage in order to use the dictionary profitably. Much excellent training has been given by using vocabulary lists gathered from all subjects in finding meaning, for alphabetical arrangement, for syllabication, and accent.

Instruction has been given on the use of the prefatory part of the dictionary to find out what it contains in the way of guide material, notes, abbreviation, rules for spelling, pluralizing, pronouncing, etc., and for the full table of symbols indicating pronunciation with respelling.

A very interesting and complete unit on a study of "How Language Began" served as a successful means of motivating dictionary study.

Another aspect of study which is essential to the effective use of books and materials is the reading of maps, diagrams, graphs, statistical tables, formulas, and the like. Through the coöperation of the other instructors, the boys make application of these tools after they have been instructed in their use during the activity period.

### III. Training in Keeping a Notebook

Students who receive systematic training in keeping a note-book during their high school courses, not only improve their high school study habits but they receive training which enables them to achieve more efficiently success in their university work.

Well organized notebooks are a decided aid to review as well as to mastery of the course. Pupils should be encouraged to keep notebooks for the filing of written papers, outlines, clippings, assignments, and other material. While it is probably poor economy, except in a few laboratory courses, to require the keeping of notebooks in a formal manner for purposes of grading, it is advisable for the teacher to suggest, guide, and criticize according to the pupil's needs. Students should not feel that notebooks are unsupervised at any time.

The first part of Saint Rita's program is training in taking notes from materials read, class lectures, and class reports. Students are trained to listen for and note only those points which he wants and needs. Note-taking in lecture periods must not be extraneous nor interfere with assimilation.

Likewise, although a wider reading program may be undertaken with profit by advanced students, the majority need that training which will help them to see what the issues are in their fields and how to center their reading about them.

The students receive training in skimming. They are taught the use of key topic-sentences, marginal, and other sub-headings, and summaries. Training in skimming through timed exercises has been found to be a successful means of increasing study ability.

Training is also given in making topical notes, marginal notes, notes in outline form, and condensed notes. The value of notes depends very definitely upon the system used. For example, some of the value depends upon the size of the unit, organization into outline, citations of source, and uniformity of notes. Definite instruction is given to prevent changing from one system to another. In such a case, however good the systems may be, the mere fact that they are not uniform prevents them from being effective. It is interesting to note that many of the boys who entered school in September without a definite system of note-taking are now making use of the essentials of a good system of notes.

Several of the elements of note taking which have been emphasized are the following:

1. Notebook—Should be loose-leaf, should be a type which can be readily opened, and the paper of uniform eight and one-half by eleven inches. This allows for revision of one page without spoiling the whole notebook; this permits classification and rearrangement of notes in the same field into one unit or arranged by topics.

Furthermore, mimeographed material can be punched and filed if a notebook is of this type.

2. Headings or Headlines—Every sheet of notes should have definite headlines to tell the source from which they are taken and the subject of which they treat. These headlines should be accurate, clear, brief, prominent, uniform in arrangement, neat and complete.

3. Form and Arrangement of the Paper—Good form and arrangement of notes means the meeting of certain standards. Those being emphasized at Saint Rita are:

(a) Notation—the lettering or numbering of each point. The system suggested is:

I
  A
    I
      a
       (1)
       (a)

The particular system of letters and numbers is not very important, but uniformity throughout a given outline is important.

(b) Indentation—Each subdivision is to be indented under the main division. It should be indented enough to show up the outline well but not so far in that the notes need be written in very short lines at the extreme right of the page. If a point requires more than one line, the second line should be indented also.

(c) Margins—Of reasonable depth on all sides but not waste of space. Condense but don't crowd.

(d) Short, concise paragraphs—Not more than three lines.

(e) Neatness—Should be neatly compiled.

(f) Use of the back of the paper—Use one side of paper only, saving the back for additions and revisions.

5. Conciseness and Brevity—Notes should be brief and to the point, yet clear and meaningful. Too full notes may lead to brain-work being replaced by mechanical copying. Be careful not to include too many details. Take down only what is important and valuable, and take that in the fewest possible words without sacrificing clearness.

During this activity period the boys receive instruction in the accepted form of written work required for every class. The following form is used:

## FORM OF WRITTEN WORK

1. Handwriting: All work to be neat and legible.
   (a) Letters distinct: dot i's, cross t's; distinguish a and o, e and i, m and w, or and u, b and k, r and n, g and y, etc.
   (b) Words: do not crowd or distort; no space inside words, equal spaces between words.
2. Write in ink, one side of the paper on regulation size paper. If you type, double space the lines.
3. Name, class, date on the first line, properly spaced.
4. Title: Skip a line above and below the title.
   (a) Where: centered, space below and above. If long, two lines, both centered.
   (b) How: first and all other words, except conjunctions, articles, prepositions, begin with capital letters. (If typed, all letters in every word a capital.)
5. Margin on both sides of paper: left side one inch; right side about half inch; gage by preceding line. No large "holes" of wavy edge.

6. Separating words: Necessary to preserve right-hand margin. Words of one syllable not separated. General rule other words: between syllables, hypen immediately after break.
7. Indent every paragraph uniformly about one inch.
8. Other pages: all but first numbered in the right-hand corner; Arabic numbers, no period after. If more than one page, use a clip to bind together.

*     *     *     *

Every technique possible is employed to prevent the students from abusing note-taking as a substitute for memory. Students see that notes taken thoughtfully and used properly will help them to remember and offer an opportunity for review instead of trying to memorize everything. Note-taking should serve as an incentive toward acquiring new material to be combined with that already accumulated.

### IV. Use of the Library

Reading plays an important part in practically all activities at Saint Rita High School. The development of appreciation and of interest in books comes rather definitely in the sphere of elementary school. Consequently, the average boy reaches high school with a friendly feeling toward books.

At high school level a steadily increased amount of independent study is required of students. Reading of intensive or study type is carried on in each subject. New fields of interest are opened up; the rate of reading increased, and there is a demand for more books to meet the wide range of individual interests stimulated in the classrooms and elsewhere.

To satisfy this expansion of interests, it is necessary to provide an abundance of good books of sufficient range of content to meet the demands of all. Such a collection can only be furnished by actual library facilities and it has been the endeavor of Saint Rita High School to open wide the doors to the field of research to show how books serve as tools, as instruments of study.

The first step in Saint Rita's program is to see that the pupil shall be able to extract the thought from the printed material. It is useless to try to do library work without this skill.

The boys are next given an understanding that the library contains a wide range of material on every subject, both recreational and informational. When the boys have developed an appreciation of the values which may be derived from the library, they are introduced to the method of making use of all facilities offered. The following types of bibliographical aids are explained to the boys so that they may make use of them.

1. *Card Catalogue*. The card catalogue of the library is organized on the same principle as a book index. The use of cross reference cards for finding related materials is explained. The method of filing a book under the title and also under the author's name is pointed out. Another feature developed is the alphabetical arrangement, placing names beginning with Mc and Mac as though they were all Mac, of Saint and St. arranged together.

2. *Special Bibliographies and Book Lists*. Although Saint Rita Students are encouraged to use the bibliographies suggested by their instructors or in their own texts, it has been deemed advisable to introduce the use of such lists of books as the *Reader's Guide*. Guides to bibliographies are also pointed out and explained.

3. *General Indexes for Magazines*. The lists for periodical literature are among the important facilities explained. Only the most outstanding, such as the *Poole Index to Periodical Literature, Reader's Guide,* and the *Annual Magazine Index,* are used for illustration.

4. *Encyclopedias and Reference Books*. The use of the *Catholic Encyclopedia, Encyclopedia Britannica, Encyclopedia Americana,* and the new *International Encyclopedia* are encouraged.

In addition to encyclopedias there is a type of reference material available which specialized in current problems. Every student should possess a knowledge and understanding of Almanacs, Year-Books, and annual Encyclopedias.

When using library books for serious study and assimilation, the same principles which apply to textbook knowledge are used.

A Librarian who is fully cognizant of these factors was selected that each boy may receive adequate attention. At present the Librarian devotes ten complete activity periods to instructing a selected group. These groups change until all pupils have a working knowledge of library technique. The following is an example which illustrates the type of outline which insures uniformity and completeness.

Library Lessons for Freshmen

*Lesson I.—Classification and Library Rules.*

1. Meaning of classification.
2. Ten main divisions.
3. Class number on book and where found.
4. Arrangement of books on the shelves, also explanation of arrangement of individual and collective biography.
5. Reference books and magazines.
6. General rules for the withdrawal of books:
   Fiction—two weeks.
   Reserve and others—overnight, due at 9:40 A. M.
   Reference books—not subject to withdrawal.
   Fines—2 cents for each day overdue on fiction.
   Fines—3 cents for each day overdue on reserve books.
   Magazines—not subject to withdrawal.

Assignment. Take a sheet of paper and write down the call number, author, and title of a book in each division of D. D. C. This necessitates a trip round the library.

*Lesson II.—Card Catalog.*

1. What the card catalog is. Compare to telephone directory.
2. Physical features.
3. Questions it answers for us:
   What books by a certain author are in the library?
   Is there a book by a certain title in the library? Where?
   What does the library contain on a certain subject?

A careful selection of topics for discussion which would serve to further the aims was made by the Director of Studies. A Council meeting was held for the purpose of determining the relative signficance and urgency of these topics.

As health and physical vigor are absolutely essential to success in high school work, it was agreed that the first activity instruction period for the upper classmen should be devoted to developing and maintaining this characteristic.

It was agreed that the presentation of each new unit be preceded by a Faculty Meeting for the purpose of clarifying by discussion, the aims, methods, and devices to be used. The Director of Studies supplies an outline of the unit and makes suggestions as to motivation, possible difficulties, and minimum accomplishment requirements.

The following Direction sheet illustrates the type of instruction given to the Moderators for instructing the students in the first unit.

### Instruction Sheet for Presenting Unit 1.

The mind is dependent upon the body for outward expression. It follows then that the normal mind will have normal and apt expression, if the instrument, the body, is normal. If the body is undeveloped, undernourished, ill-cared for, the mind will not find fitting expression. In inferior bodies, the mind becomes dormant and not alert, dull and not keen, ill-tempered and not eventempered.

To develop a sound body, care about bodily needs must be considered. Compare the body to a machine and have your class make a table, comparing the phases of a boy's life to the "life" of a machine, e. g.:

|   | | Boy | Machine |
|---|---|---|---|
| A. | Rest | Needs eight hours | Must rest to allow it to cool |
| B. | Food | Proper food | Right oil and lubricants |
| C. | | | |
| D. | | | |

4. Kinds of cards in the catalog, and information given. Author—title—subject. Guide cards.
5. Filing rules to help in finding a book:
   "A," "AN" and "THE" are disregarded.
   Short words come before long. Example: "Book" "bookkeeping."

Assignment. Look in the card catalog and find an author and subject card. Draw a picture of each using red pencil block capitals where you think necessary.

### Lesson III.—The Physical Book.

1. Purpose of the lesson—to use books skillfully by the knowledge of their various parts.
2. Various parts of a book—super, sections, title page, preface, table of contents, list of maps or illustrations, introductions, text, appendix and index.

### Lesson IV.—Reference Books.

Encyclopedias. What they are and how arranged. Time to be spent in going around library with class giving suggestions and answering questions.

\*　　\*　　\*　　\*　　\*

Having received adequate training and guidance during their first and second year activity periods, the Junior and Senior boys should require little assistance in study techniques. Their meetings with the Moderator during the activity periods are therefore devoted to the development of proper character traits and correct attitudes of citizenship and Christianity. The placement of training of this type in the latter years of a student's education followed much consideration of the values therein. The apparently logical arrangement was to have this type of guidance follow the orientation of the student to the field of acquiring knowledge. Once the boys are well established in the methods of independent study, they can more readily grasp the significance of materials presented to them for personality development.

After the students have submitted to you their tables, you may amplify and explain further:

1. The need of proper rest.
   Lack of rest brings about nervous disorders, irritability, bad temper.
2. Care of clothing.
   Shoes shined, clean and unwrinkled ties, spotted clothing, needless exposure to the elements, broken shoe laces, soiled shirts, buttons off clothing, holes in the heels of socks. Remind students that they must acquire the habit of neatness and develop good taste in clothes, for later on, their future position in life depends upon a good appearance. It is accepted and proved by professional men that a good appearance is 75 per cent of success.
3. A complete change of clothes, accompanied by a shower or bath is advised twice a week, at least. Pimples and unsightly blackheads are caused by not bathing at close intervals.
4. Teeth. Care for them by brushing them properly; have them cleaned by your dentist twice a year. Defects in teeth develop an inferiority complex. Bad teeth cause organic disorders. An ounce of prevention, etc.
5. Discuss the value of exercise, but stress that too much violent exercise is also the cause of ill-health.

Have your class write a composition concerning their care of the body. Tell the students not to sign their names. Then discuss each paper and draw up a health schedule for your class. Explain that habits once formed are not easily forgotten.

A similar outline of each unit is made by the Director of Studies in order to assure uniformity of achievement by securing uniformity of presentation.

At each subsequent monthly meeting of the Faculty, a decision is reached concerning the subject of instruction for the following month. It has been found that this method of permitting variation of topics provides for adapting the subjects to the immediate requirements of the student body.

The individuals who maintain their well-being through their own efforts are interested also in those forms of community cleanliness, sanitation, and well-being which will promote the general welfare.

In like manner, individuals who through receiving guidance in Religion as a solid basis for a philosophy of living which will aid in solving man's deepest questions and satisfying his deepest needs, formulate a true Catholic idealism, will continue the struggle to increase the ideals and varied manifestations of Christianity throughout the world. If the regeneration of mankind and the bringing of the Kingdom of God to the world is to be accomplished, then a supreme effort must be made toward training in ethical character and toward human relationships carried on as an evidence of the better operation of religious influences.

To further these aims, and objectives, the Junior and Senior students receive definite training on Catholic Ideals, for the development of an appreciation of how much joy there is in a life of self-sacrifice and service, in a life of more intelligently knowing and practicing more faithfully the Catholic ideal of life.

This is being accomplished through the assignment of units on the Catholic ideal of life based on the Commandments as duties of love of God and neighbor. The topics selected for development are chosen for study as the felt need arises as previously stated. The first of these units, that is of Health and Physical Well-Being, has already been discussed. The second unit is Common Politeness. This outline was given to each teacher to follow for the months of November and December.

## COMMON POLITENESS

*To Teachers:*

1. Loud talking in classrooms.
2. Throwing of missiles of any form.
3. Entering classroom before teacher as he opens the door.

4. Raucous laughter.
5. Addressing laymen with omission of "Sir" or "Mister."
6. Rushing for door at conclusion of period.
7. Distracting teacher by asking knowingly a foolish question.
8. Talking while the teacher is lecturing or explaining.
9. Accepting any papers, reprimands, etc., without saying: "Thank you," Sir or Father.
10. Removing hats while speaking to teacher or carrying of hats to the class rooms.
11. All classes to stand if a visitor, the Principal, or teacher enters the classroom.
12. Referring to the time repeatedly.

*To Other Students:*

1. Eliminate pushing and shoving.
2. Don't yell to boy twenty feet away.
3. Making fun of your classmates if they fail to respond in recitations.
4. Avoid using odious nicknames.
5. Avoid expressing too strong feelings.

*To the Family:*

1. Addressing parents, use proper respect.
2. Never speak disparagingly about them.
3. Preserve a certain approved etiquette at your meals.
4. Never talk back to them.
5. Go out of your way to perform little acts of kindness to them.

Formulate a list of qualities that everyone should possess to be classified as a Christian Gentleman.

These outlined topics are not complete in themselves. Each teacher may add what he thinks is necessary and eliminate such items which may not need to be stressed. The other topics which are to be considered the basic curriculum for achieving the aims are Obedience, Sobriety, Honesty, Gratitude, Trustworthiness, Vocations, etc.

Each of these topics is considered from the point of view of its relationship to God, to self, and to others. For example, in studying what practical religion is, the students first discuss the meaning of religion; second, the reasons for exhibiting this virtue in daily life and the opportunities that high school students have for practicing religion through prayer, self-denial, abstinence, and observances of Sundays and holydays, at home, at school, at church, with members of their families and with fellow students. Students are encouraged to read numerous biographies to note examples of the various virtues practiced by the great men and women who took their religion out of the field of theory and carried it into the field of reality. Religious education is the antidote for Communism and agnostic philosophy which are the common enemies of religion today.

Closely allied to religion is good citizenship. The need of the students for guidance in citizenship is great; the International and the Federal problems of the United States, State and Municipal problems are so extensive and of such complexity that being an American citizen is both comprehensive and difficult.

We do not propose to claim that guidance in citizenship will solve these problems, nor that any school activity will directly help them. It is obviously certain however, that until students begin doing things that, at least, closely resemble the activities involved in the solution of these problems, there is no likelihood that they will be prepared for even the simplest tasks of citizenship which they must assume as adults. It is also evident that just as problems of agreement and control grow out of many organized activities,—homes, recreation, health, industry, agriculture, commerce, and transportation,—therefore the students' opportunity to learn agreement and control needs the environment of organized youth-life activities. Successful citizenship is an art; it requires practice under guidance in order to be learned.

The activities needed for developing citizenship as they are provided for by the Moderator and the desired outcome of the activities are:

1. Discussing important issues in school citizenship and out-

side government. Reading newspapers with a critical attitude; judging campaign speeches and literature; obtaining facts on parties, laws, candidates, and public questions; using historical data; considering probable future effects of alternative decisions.

2. Learning the value and wisdom back of the following methods and the results to be accomplished through the use of argument, disagreement, agreement, and compromising on important civic questions with due consideration for right and with tolerance for differing opinions.

3. Developing an understanding of the technique of committee work by serving on committees, conferring, formulating plans, and writing reports.

4. Developing an understanding of the value of coöperation with other citizens and with officers for the safety and proper care of life and property, and for the execution of laws.

5. An understanding of needs and values of contributing to good citizenship and public welfare by doing more than one's share toward cleanliness, order, and safety, reporting dangers, abuses, and infractions.

6. Development of the realization that majority rule is needed and necessary, and an acquiescent attitude to the will of the majority, while preserving minority rights.

7. Develop an appreciation of the value of obedience to laws and rules, complying with traffic and other regulations.

8. An appreciation of the reasons for protecting and using rightly all public property.

9. Encouraging the selection of citizenship questions of current interest and bringing such to the attention of the group for comparison and evaluation.

Finally, while our outline of subject matter for the study of citizenship is admittedly sketchy, it is of sufficient breadth to indicate that the aim is not to parallel the activities of the civics class. It is hoped that the point has been made clear that the objective is that of fitting the student for governmental coöperation.

As the felt need for the other topics arise, the Faculty will meet to discuss the method to be used in order to secure their achievement.

The Faculty agree that the purpose of this guidance plan is that the students may learn to live better lives. Our guidance curriculum is formulated solely of the things which life itself requires; quality of activity is stressed, not quantity; student initiative is of great importance as a criterion of guidance, both for the group and the individual. *Self-Guidance* is the final aim.

All this is done to further the scholastic efforts and increase the knowledge of student skills. In addition to the description and evaluation of the newer significant techniques being employed in managing the diagnostic and remedial procedures, a brief account of other effective techniques being employed to raise scholastic standards, to enrich the curriculum and to develop lasting interests is herewith appended.

I. *The Technical Course.* The major revision made in the program of studies during the past year was the introduction of a technical course of study. The rapid industrial and social changes since the beginning of the present century have led to reorganization in secondary education throughout the country. The needs of adolescent youth grow out of the conditions of modern life. Our young people need training which will equip them for active and intelligent participation in those social groups of which they are now members and of which they are likely to become members. It is vitally important that our schools recognize the dynamic, ever-changing nature of civilization. It was in recognition of this importance that Saint Rita High School instituted the first Catholic Technical High School in Chicago.

II. *Subjects added to the Program of Studies.* In addition to the inauguration of a Technical Course of Study, several suggestions were made and accepted by the Faculty for curricular expansion. This program of curricular expansion includes the introduction of classes in Biology, Catholic Sociology, classes in Music for which credit is given, and Economics.

(a) *Biology.* There are few subjects in the high school program of studies that have greater possibilities for practical application than the Biological Sciences. Newspapers and periodicals are replete with references to animal and plant life, human health, nature, evolution and the like. Biology has a practical value to agriculture, home-making, and other occupations, through a knowledge of rodent and insect life, plants, foods and growth, soil fertilization, germs, and bacteria.

Some pupils should receive from the study of Biology a preparation for advanced study in hygiene, sanitation, medicine, agriculture, psychology, or philosophy.

It appears safe to mention that all persons ought to know the simple facts and processes in the growth of plants and animals. This kind of knowledge is valuable to all pupils who have yards to care for, also for recreation in nature, and for home-making and vocational use.

(b) *Sociology.* As the science which treats of the social relations of human beings and of their entire social life with the view of promoting social welfare, Catholic Sociology is acknowledged to be an essential part of Saint Rita's Program of Studies.

Sociology studies social evils only as they are a part of social life. It concentrates on the study of the higher social relationships resulting from or tending to shape political, economic, or religious life. Sociology searches into man's aptitudes, characteristics and virtues; it studies the family, the State, and the church. The objective aim or purpose of sociology is temporal happiness or welfare. The Catholic sociological viewpoint, as evidenced in the aims of Sociology, as taught at Saint Rita High School does not neglect the higher end of man.

It is the desire of Saint Rita High School to inculcate in the students a knowledge and understanding of their duties toward God and their fellow man which are founded on immutable principles which in their essence do not change. Such knowledge is necessary in order that Catholic students may meet with proper appreciation and understanding the teachings of a non-Catholic world which regards philosophy and morality as something changeable and subject to tradition and evolution. The dangers of becoming a victim of false views are considerably lessened if students leave high school with a realization of the guiding principles of right and wrong, and a guiding purpose of securing the welfare and happiness of the individual, the family and community.

(c) *Music.* There is no subject in the entire program of studies that has been the cause of such widespread controversy in recent years as that of school-sponsored musical training. There are still those critics of an older generation who would like to see music eliminated from the school program as an unnecessary subject.

Saint Rita School Faculty not only have concluded that school music is one of the fundamental phases of curricular structure but in cognizance of this fact also have granted music a place in the list of credit-bearing subjects. This decision may be readily justified.

Music is intimately connected with our everyday life. From earliest childhood, music has a familiar and home-like aspect and it is as natural for most boys to sing as it is to speak their native tongue.

Music is of highly cultural value. While other subjects possess cultural value also, music of all the arts, is the most exalted and the most idealized because it is the most spiritual.

Music has established a place of importance in secondary schools. It is the responsibility of every school, in every way possible, to furnish, to its pupils, activities which they may utilize profitably and wisely in the increased amount of leisure time. The study of music to an unusual degree affords a wise outlet for the use of increased leisure time.

The avocational possibilities of music can hardly be surpassed by any other school activity. We have just begun to realize the uses to which music may be devoted as a pleasurable and profitable avocation. There is no good reason why the work in band and orchestra and vocal music, so wisely begun in school years, should cease when our pupils become active citizens in the community. Saint Rita Band and Orchestra are examples of outstanding accomplishments in Chicago.

Unless we continue this work, which is of such great importance to our young people, we are not fulfilling our duties toward complete training for future citizenship. Long after our pupils have forgotten the lessons which they have learned from the more traditional subjects, they will continue to enjoy and utilize their work in music, and it will prove to be of lasting value, not only to themselves but to the community in which they live.

Inasmuch as music is necessary to the educational needs of the twentieth century, greater percentages of students may be assured of being introduced to the æsthetic, creative, disciplinary, emotional and ethical use of leisure time, to physical, social and vocational objectives, if all educators will agree that music education is as worthy of being accredited as any other subject in the program of studies. It is at the present time at Saint Rita School.

The outstanding work now being done in this field at Saint Rita School has already made a pronounced contribution to student and community welfare by developing a unified group consciousness, and an appreciation of music and how to produce it.

(d) *Economics.* Character building is best secured through the study of social sciences since character is so largely a matter of social relationships. The study of Political Economy as one branch of the social sciences serves to lay down principles of thought and action by which man's character can be improved.

The subject matter of Economics as presented at Saint Rita School is a study of human activity in its relation to the wealth-producing factors of the world. The activity of man as well as the end of that activity must be considered. The aim of the study of Economics is to obtain knowledge of wealth, of its production, distribution, and consumption through a study of the various peoples in their efforts to acquire wealth, the various moral and physical agents which influence the increase or decrease of wealth, and the various factors of land, labor, capital, exchange, social organizations, money, trade, property, and the correlations that exist among them.

The subject matter therefore considers the relations of men among themselves and the relations of men with the external world in their pursuit of material goods. The subject matter is therefore threefold:

1. Man as a social being, bound by the moral law and destined to eternal life in the supernatural order.

2. The external world governed by concrete laws.

3. Human activity, or the relation between man and the material things upon which he exercises his activity.

The broad principles or desirable objectives are: (1) Knowledge of State legislation, wise, moderate and progressive. (2) An understanding of the action and influence of the Church and Christian Charity. (3) An understanding of individual and associated initiative.

The study of Political Economy is usually divided into the historical, the theoretical, and the practical part.

The historical part of Political Economy is the study of the progress of a nation and the causes affecting Political Economy.

The theoretical Political Economy studies the principles of wealth, value, price, exchange, distribution, consumption, and production.

The practical part of Political Economy takes up the actual applications of the theories studied under theoretical Economy, and in addition, studies the questions of taxation, free trade and protection, banking, insurance, corporations, and the labor problems.

The practical training for participation in citizenship activities in life outside the school which is accomplished through the study of Political Economy may well be considered justification for including this subject in the Saint Rita Program of Studies.

III. *Program of Supervised Study.* Along with gaining an understanding of the theory of study, pupils also need to be taught how to apply this theory so as to produce effective work. Pupils vary in the amount of specific training in study that they need. The ideal always is to develop the ability of independent study, and the quicker this condition is reached the better. Pupils of high intelligence as well as poorer students are materially helped by an analysis of the study situation into its elements and presenting these elements to the class. That is teaching pupils how to study by giving them a complete understanding of the factors involved. This is helpful to all students. The fact that study habits are quickly acquired makes it desirable, if not necessary, that teaching pupils how to study parallels the use of books.

The administrative organization of Saint Rita School has, therefore, revised the schedules for the lengthened class period form of supervised study. Instructors fully realize that the study time should never be cut short by prolonging the recitation time. Another important factor is that class time must be a learning, not a lesson hearing period.

It has been found that the concentrated twenty to twenty-five minute supervised study period will secure more real learning than the assumed but often hypothetical hour or two spent in home study without direction.

The fifty-minute period is never rigidly divided. (The ideal period of sixty full minutes was the original plan but because of the religious schedule it had to be abandoned.) The suggestion to the Faculty is that ten minutes be devoted to testing or review, fifteen or twenty minutes to assignment, and twenty or twenty-five minutes to supervised study. (This method only applies to the assignment recitation plan.) Lesson-hearing as such may be almost entirely eliminated. Supervised study properly conducted, reduces the necessity for the recitation. It is pupil activity that is needed for learning, not teacher activity. Supervised study is pupil activity in its most advantageous form. There are times when it may be well to give most of the class time to explaining the assignment or to supervised study with an occasional halting of the work for oral or written testing. In some cases the assignment needs very little explanation, and then most of the time can be given to supervised study. This program of organization of the supervised study period is closely allied to the work done by the Moderators in directing study habits during the activity period. The improvement of results has proved to be an edifying evidence of success for this plan. It has also increased the powers of initiative and self-reliance in the students.

*IV. Home Study.* Attention to supervised study in its present form may be considered a direct outgrowth of the poor results obtained from home study. Conditions for study in many homes are very poor. The child is placed in the position of coping with various distractions of the home to the detriment of accomplishments.

Another problem is that having been assigned homework by several instructors in one evening the student finds himself so overburdened that he must decide whether to give scant attention to all assignments or do well certain assignments, leaving others completely undone.

In respect to the available time of pupils, it is necessary to remember that many of the students are working after school, that others are taking private music lessons or private instruction in other subjects and that all students should have relaxation in the open air at least two hours a day, participate in the activities of their families, and go to bed at a reasonable hour.

Home study should and does require pedagogical attention. Properly administered home study is a desirable activity. Of first importance is the formulation of a schedule whereby students are assured assignments of reasonable lengths each day. In order to secure system in this regard, a committee of three faculty members apportioned the subjects for home study on different days, as the following schedule illustrates.

### GENERAL HOME STUDY ASSIGNMENT DAYS

#### *I. Freshmen*

Monday—English, General Science.
Tuesday—Algebra, Latin.
Wednesday—History, English.
Thursday, General Science, Algebra.
Friday—Latin, Religion, History.

#### *II. Sophomores*

Monday—English, Latin.
Tuesday—Geometry, Religion.

Wednesday—Latin, English.
Thursday—Biology, Geometry, Economics.
Friday—Religion, Latin.

### III. Juniors

Monday—English, Commercial Law.
Tuesday—Spanish, French, Latin.
Wednesday—Physics, English.
Thursday—Spanish, French, Commercial Law and Latin.
Friday—Physics, Religion.

### IV. Seniors

Monday—English, Spanish, French, Latin.
Tuesday—Chemistry, Stenography.
Wednesday—Math., History, English.
Thursday—Spanish, French, Latin, Chemistry.
Friday—Math., Stenography, Sociology.

The rule is laid down that all homework should be done independently; that no personal help from members of the family or fellow students should be accepted. All basic teaching should be done by the teacher in school. That leaves drill and memory work, application exercises, supplementary reading, reading in Literature, and composition work which may be done at home. Students of lesser intelligence are encouraged to seek from their teachers re-teaching if they cannot perform home assignments. This desired support between teacher and student is a stimulus for independence. The homework problem as now administered at Saint Rita School is a profitable activity for the student, not merely a haphazard procedure.

V. *Student Council.* The guidance plan favors the teaching of knowledge and ideals by the laboratory method just as the laboratory plan is used in fashioning teachers.

The theory which must be upheld in this community is that if student participation in school government is permitted, then the practice of this must be real, not staged.

The following are a few considerations which were thought over by the Faculty:

(a) Setting—The school must be organized on a student participation plan before the student council is organized.

(b) Classroom preparations—Free discussion in the homeroom will prove an asset in making a plan of student participation a success.

(c) Good student activities—A good program of activities will prevent the Student Council from attempting to meddle in matters best handled by the teachers.

(d) Pupil initiative—Plans should not be adopted by the students until they receive confirmation by the Student Council and Faculty.

(e) Government must be by the students—Students must be ready to support their officers and help to enforce their own laws.

(f) There must be a feeling of confidence and support between Faculty and Student Government.

(g) The Student Council should follow school needs and be guided by the school problems.

The following is the organization of Saint Rita High School Student Council. It evolves from the Honor Society. Each member of the Student Council is a member of the Honor Society. The chairman of the Honor Society is elected by the members while the chairman of the Student Council is appointed by a faculty committee consisting of the Principal, the Director of Studies, and the Director of Youth Guidance. The chairmen of the Honor Society and Student Council work hand in hand in carrying out the will of the students. The students are represented by a spokesman who is elected from the Activity group.

Committees are formed at various times during the year; some are of a permanent nature while others are formed only for the length of time for which they may be needed. The following items are concerned with this student administration:

1. Welfare: Preserving order in the corridors and stairways, lunchroom.

2. Education: School affairs, scholarship exams., reception and direction of visitors.

3. Organization: Minor activities and clubs.

4. Entertainment: Social affairs.

5. Publications: School papers, Year Book, Publicity.

The Student Council has served to assist our boys in finding a standard of conduct for themselves and to provide penalties for violators.

VI. *Saint Rita Honor Society.* Saint Rita Honor Society is a chapter of the National Honor Society of Secondary Schools, having become affiliated with them in March, 1936.

The copy of the Constitution of the Society sets forth the aims, composition and membership.

## CONSTITUTION OF THE SAINT RITA CHAPTER OF THE NATIONAL HONOR SOCIETY OF SECONDARY SCHOOLS

### ARTICLE I. NAME AND PURPOSE

*Section 1.* The name of this chapter shall be the Saint Rita Chapter of the National Honor Society of Secondary Schools.

*Section 2.* The object of this chapter shall be to create an enthusiasm for scholarship, to stimulate a desire to render service, to promote worthy leadership, and to encourage the development of character in pupils of Saint Rita High School.

### ARTICLE II. MEMBERSHIP

*Section 1.* Membership of this chapter shall be known as active and graduate. The graduate members have no vote.

*Section 2.* Membership of this chapter shall be based on scholarship, service, leadership, and character.

*Section 3.* Candidates eligible to election in this chapter shall stand in the first third of their respective classes in scholarship. They shall have spent at least one year in Saint Rita High School.

*Section 4.* Not more than ten of the Senior class shall be elected to this chapter.

*Section 5.* The election of not more than five of the second semester Junior class may take place during their semester of eligibility for candidacy.

*Section 6.* Any member of the faculty may propose to the council the names of students eligible for membership in this chapter through the faculty moderator. Two-thirds vote shall be necessary to carry any member.

*Section 7.* Any active member who falls below the standards which were the basis for his election to membership shall be dropped from the chapter by a majority vote of the student council. The evidence must be stated clearly before the assembled body before any such vote is taken.

*Section 8.* If so dropped, his emblem shall be returned to the president of this chapter.

## ARTICLE III. COUNCIL

*Section 1.* The faculty shall be represented in the Student Council by a moderator.

*Section 2.* This moderator shall be chosen from among the following faculty members: The Principal, Prefect of Study, the Disciplinarian and the Chaplain.

## ARTICLE IV. OFFICERS

*Section 1.* The officers of this chapter shall be a president, vice-president, secretary, and treasurer.

*Section 2.* No student shall serve as an officer for more than one semester.

*Section 3.* A majority of votes cast shall be necessary to elect any officer of this chapter. If the first vote does not yield a majority, a second vote shall be taken on the candidates who have received the highest number of votes.

*Section 4.* It shall be the duty of the president to preside at the meetings of this chapter.

*Section 5.* The vice-president shall fill the chair of the president in his absence.

*Section 6.* The secretary shall keep the minutes of meetings, a record of all business, and all records filed.

*Section 7.* The treasurer shall be elected from among the members of the council, shall receive and disburse all funds of the chapter and shall keep an accurate account of all receipts and disbursements.

*Section 8.* Two officers, a chairman and a treasurer, shall be elected at the last meeting of the school term, to serve protem until such time as the regular officers for the following semester are elected.

*Section 9.* The secretary also shall certify to the secretary of the National Council the number graduated in each class, and the names of those elected to membership in this chapter.

## ARTICLE V. EXECUTIVE COMMITTEE

*Section 1.* The executive committee shall consist of the faculty moderator and the officers of the chapter.

*Section 2.* The executive committee shall have general charge of the meetings and business of the chapter, but any action on the part of the executive committee may be subject to review of the chapter.

## ARTICLE VI. FACULTY SUPERVISION

*Section 1.* The activities of this chapter shall be subject to the approval of the principal.

## ARTICLE VII. MEETINGS

*Section 1.* The regular meetings of this chapter shall be held weekly.

*Section 2.* The first regular meeting of each semester shall be for the election of officers.

*Section 3.* Special meetings, approved by the moderator, may be held under call of the president.

*Section 4.* All meetings shall be open meetings and shall be held under sponsorship of the moderator.

*Section 5.* This chapter shall conduct its meetings according to Roberts' *Rules of Order,* in all points not expressly provided for in the Constitution of this chapter.

### Article VIII. Emblem

*Section 1.* Each member of this chapter shall be entitled to wear the emblem adopted by the National Society, which he will receive upon payment of its cost.

*Section 2.* Any member who withdraws or is dropped from the chapter shall return the emblem to the chapter and be reimbursed for it.

### Article IX. Dues

*Section 1.* Each member of this chapter shall contribute monthly a sum the amount of which shall be decided upon by the members of the council.

### Article X. Amendments

*Section 1.* This Constitution may be amended by a two-thirds vote of the chapter, provided that the proposed amendment has been approved by the moderator and notice to members has been given at least two weeks previous to the meeting at which it is to be voted upon. All amendments must be approved by the National Council.

\*     \*     \*     \*

The student members have been permitted the use of one room, which they have furnished as a clubroom. Honor students are permitted to go to the clubroom during their study periods or whenever they have completed the advance assignments for the day.

Permission to spend portions of the day in a pleasantly furnished comfortable place of their own, in which they may read or enjoy themselves otherwise is a most powerful incentive to other students to secure membership which requires accomplishment in scholarship, character development, service to the school, students and faculty, and qualities of leadership. This is indeed a growing and worth while institution which Saint Rita's Faculty is proud of.

VII. *Health Service.* The Health Service at Saint Rita includes several administrative procedures designed to determine the physical status of the student, to inform parents of the defects that may be present and help in every way in the prevention of disease and in the correction of defects.

Health Service in the school is primarily an educational effort working toward the maximum possible physical development of each individual pupil. Health and physical education comprise an integral part of training for citizenship.

(a) *Care of Visual Defects.* At the beginning of the school term a corp of three oculists made a completely thorough, professionally accurate examination of the visual abilities of every student in the school. Parents were notified of each defect and requested to act upon the notification at once. It was most edifying to find the large percentage of parents who immediately assumed responsibility for having the defects corrected.

(b) *Dental Hygiene.* Every student in the school was given a careful examination by the school dentist. In correlation with this work, the moderators took care of the notifying of the parents of these who are in this Activity Group.

This procedure has combined to improve the health of students as well as their scholastic standing. Parents demand particular attention from private schools more so than from public schools. This personal touch has assured the parents of the great interest that each teacher has for his students.

VIII. *Saturday Class.* During the first month of the current semester, various faculty members reported that many of the students were not achieving maximum success despite the fact that they were possessed of excellent native ability. Investigations made by the moderators disclosed that there was a close connection between those who were troublesome disciplinary cases and those who were avoiding the responsibility of completing assignments. The Faculty agreed that obviously some treatment of these cases on non-coöperative delinquents was needed.

It was decided that any treatment of such delinquents should necessarily strike at the pupil through depriving him of a pleasurable experience and through arousing the interest of the home influences. The organization of a class to meet on Saturday morning wherein such students would be compelled to perform definite work assignments served the purpose. A record of each student whose name appeared on this list is inscribed in a record book for future reference. This record book is kept in the office so that moderators may use it for their accumulative records.

Each instructor who recommends that a student attend the Saturday class makes the assignment and is asked to "look in" Saturday morning to see if his students are progressing in the given assignments.

The following schedule of teacher assignment and instructions will clarify this administration problem:

### NOTICE

Please announce this Saturday Study to your classes and explain the purpose behind it. Request each one to bring at least three textbooks, pencil, and paper. Inform the pupil that there will be absolute silence although from 10:25 to 10:35, time will be given to attend to their personal needs. This study class will meet in the Library.

1. The teacher will report to the office those pupils whom he dispenses from this Study Class so that the office may check his name from the book.
2. The Supervisor of Studies shall read on Friday the list of students eligible for the Saturday Class.
3. The teacher in charge shall report all absentees to the office of the Supervisor of Studies. If the door to the office is closed then slip your list under the door. Please do this promptly so that an immediate check-up may be made on Monday morning.
4. The complete schedule of priests and laymen is given to you that, if you discover that you cannot be present on your day, you may exchange places with another teacher.

IX. *Faculty Meetings.* Faculty meetings are held on the last Friday afternoon of each month. All the instructors are expected to be present for the purpose of discussing principles of organization and administration of topics relative to the welfare of the entire Faculty and student body. There occurs also a coöperative discussion for diagnosing the particular difficulties of individual students. Each moderator is prepared to give his diagnosis of a discussed pupil to his other instructors who may profit from this given information.

All teachers know the unsatisfactory nature of faculty meetings where issues are presented suddenly without any previous information and study. To obviate this difficulty, a notice is posted in the Faculty Room where all teachers may write the problems which they wish to discuss at the meeting.

X. *Award of Merit.* The awards of merit are gold and silver certificates awarded to students who have been achieving remarkable scholastic success. Students having a straight "A" average in all subjects receive a gold certificate at the end of each quarter. Students having grades of "A" and "B" in their subjects receive the silver certificate. The fourth year student having the greatest number of gold and silver certificates (one gold certificate is equal to two silver), will be awarded a gold excellency medal at graduation.

This method of awarding scholastic achievement is a powerful means of motivation to the boys. Parents of students receiving these awards are likely to become more friendly toward the school and the faculty.

The Faculty of Saint Rita High School feel that the program of guidance as administered during the past year has brought each division of the school success in developing the abilities and skills which should be acquired at each successive level.

The results of the efforts which have been briefly described have shown themselves not merely in objective measures of improvement in specific skills but in more adequate adjustment and satisfying advancement in the subsequent grades of the pupils with whom the Faculty have worked. The direction of study in the High School is increasingly a positive development of new methods of work on higher levels rather than a partial remedial effort to correct weaknesses persisting in the Elementary School.

The Faculty of Saint Rita High School respectfully submit the opinion that the summary of the program of organization and administration as previously described is responsible for the efficiency of Saint Rita High School, by the Grace of God and the saintly assistance of Saint Augustine and Saint Rita.

The Saint Rita program (1) effectively embraces a practical philosophy of secondary education; (2) provides an educational program which is adequate to the needs of all; (3) includes a comprehensive scheme of social training; (4) articulates with the lower and higher schools; (5) provides for the individual difference; (6) affords a continuous, comprehensive program of guidance; (7) utilizes the service facilities; (8) approaches maximum utilization of pupil and educational personnel; (9) has developed an efficient program of supervision and professional growth.

Let us earnestly pray that students shall continue to be made morally, mentally, and socially ready to take their place in society, to work for the common good, and to work out their eternal salvation when they leave Saint Rita High.

One final word concerning the pupil and the teacher. Every school desires to develop and graduate a good student but how may we characterize a good student? The following outline suggests characteristics which good students should possess:

### Characteristics of Good Students—Standards of Attainment

1. *He makes sure that he understands the assignment.*
   (a) He makes written notes on the assignment.
   (b) He makes a preliminary inspection of the work to see that he understands what he is to do.
   (c) He asks for further explanation if assignment is not clear or asks the teacher to repeat directions.
   (d) He tries to see the purpose of the assignment and to relate it to the whole course or parts of the course.

(e) He keeps a record of his assignments in a part of his notebook especially reserved for this purpose.

2. *He plans a definite study schedule both as to time and place.*
   (a) If possible, he studies in a place especially reserved for this purpose and used for no other purposes.
   (b) He sets aside a certain time for study each day.
   (c) He starts to work promptly.
       (1) He starts his study on the same subject each day.
       (2) He reviews rapidly the previous lesson.
   (d) He does his work regularly day after day.
   (e) He does not allow outside disturbances to interrupt his work.

3. *He decides on the proper method of study to follow.*
   (a) If directions are given, he follows them exactly.
   (b) If no directions are given, he decides on the proper method of study to follow.
       (1) He decides if facts are to be memorized.
       (2) Raises questions on material presented.
       (3) Summarizes main ideas.
       (4) Obtains information for solving problems or answering questions or writing reports.
       (5) Prepares an outline.
       (6) Preparing an oral or written report, etc.
       (7) Makes diagrams or tables, etc.
   (c) He varies his rate of reading according to the type of material and purpose for which he is reading.
   (d) He has definite techniques for carrying out the various types of study activities.

4. *He gets ready the necessary study material.*
   (a) Locates assignment in textbook.
   (b) Determines topics or headings under which materials may be found.
   (c) Uses card catalogue to locate new sources of material.
   (d) Uses index and table of contents to locate material on specific topics.

(e) Whenever possible he gathers facts through direct observation.

(f) He gets ideas from others through discussion or asking questions.

5. *He wants to learn.*

(a) He comes to school because he realizes the worth of an education to him rather than because he is sent by his parents.

(b) He tries to become interested in subjects which are initially uninteresting.

(c) He uses his school experiences to interpret the world in which he lives.

(d) He decides upon his purpose in life and studies with this end in view.

(e) If he is not interested he asks his instructor for reasons for present work.

(f) He talks with others who are interested to discover new sources of interest.

6. *He reviews his ideas after they have been discussed in class.*

(a) He talks over his lessons with classmates and parents.

(b) He constructs or revises outlines or summaries after the material has been discussed in class.

(c) He looks over examination papers and discusses incorrect answers with his teacher.

(d) He keeps systematic outlines of work covered to serve as a basis for review.

(e) He reviews at frequent intervals the work which has been covered in light of the new material which has been presented.

7. *He is as independent as he can profitably be.*

(a) He does not ask the teacher or others for help until he is certain that he can go no further without assistance.

(b) He does not wait to be told how to do everything.

(c) He works out new ways of doing things, exercising his own originality and individuality.

(d) He tries various ways of expressing ideas by finding new examples, drawings, pictures, stories, etc., to illustrate his points.

(e) He stands up for his own ideas if they are based on adequate data.

(f) He is not afraid to ask about what he does not understand.

(g) He makes up back work without prompting from the teacher.

8. *He is an active participant in class exercises.*

(a) He asks intelligent questions.

(b) He supplies illustrations and examples to illustrate ideas presented in class.

(c) He suggests new ways of doing things.

(d) He suggests new sources of information.

(e) He is alert to each question asked by the teacher—he answers the questions mentally to himself.

(f) He volunteers freely without being called upon.

(g) He accepts good, clear-cut evidence without useless argument.

9. *He makes constant effort to increase his vocabulary.*

(a) He realizes that his thinking is largely determined by the meanings which he has acquired.

(b) When he encounters new words he adds them to his vocabulary by practicing using the words.

(c) He reads extensively to acquire vicarious experiences and to build up his stock of meanings.

(d) He explores various fields of knowledge to secure new intellectual contacts of a specific sort.

(e) He constantly puts into words the meanings he has acquired.

(f) He looks up new words in the dictionary, learning pronunciation as well as meaning.

(g) He studies the derivation of words.

  (h)  He studies the finer meanings of words.
  (i)  He courts criticism on the use which he makes of words.

10.  *He reflects before he answers questions or does exercises.*
  (a)  He does not accept the first suggestion that comes to his mind.
  (b)  He regards suggestions as tentative and proceeds to test them.
  (c)  He examines the inferences of his hypotheses.
  (d)  He avoids the tendency to jump to conclusions.
  (e)  He gives evidence for his inferences.

11.  *He maintains a critical attitude towards material studied and toward his own beliefs.*
  (a)  He finds contraditions and inaccuracies.
  (b)  He discovers if conclusions are based on facts or opinions.
  (c)  He compares viewpoints of different authorities.
  (d)  He seeks information on both sides of questions.
  (e)  He questions statements which he reads or hears and seeks to justify them before accepting them as true.
  (f)  He is willing to change his beliefs if the evidence warrants.
  (g)  He criticizes his own work.
  (h)  He looks below the surface of a problem, finding reasons to account for the facts.
  (i)  He shows the ability to distinguish between authorities which are reliable and those that are not.
  (j)  He takes criticism kindly and attempts to profit by it.

*          *          *          *

In conclusion, it must be stated that the teacher is the most important cog in the educational process, for the teacher really is the school.  It is the teacher who makes the curriculum, who plans the activities, who guides the pupil, who selects the materials by means of which this educational process goes on.  It is the teacher's example which motivates pupil activity and develops pupil attitudes. If there is anyone who can understand a pupil, it is the teacher who is constantly in the pupil's society, supervising, admonishing, guiding, directing, diagnosing strengths and weaknesses, consoling, sympathizing, and encouraging. There is no aspect of the entire range of the student's life that the teacher does not touch and we at Saint Rita's have made that range complete by the introduction of our present moderator system which insures a greater understanding between the teacher and pupil. The reasons that a pupil comes to Saint Rita High School are numerous and diverse; the reasons that he desires to stay at Saint Rita's are measured by the love, respect and esteem which he has for his teachers!